150% Better Auditions:
Using Mindfulness Practice to Improve Your Acting

KEVIN PAGE

150% PERCENT BOOKS

DEDICATION

To the teachers, casting directors, directors, crew members, agents and managers, other cast members, and stars who have made my career on stage and screen a miraculous journey.

CONTENTS

ACKNOWLEDGMENTS

Thanks to my family, who have put up with my multiple creative incarnations (including writer). My publicist, Joanne McCall, for convincing me to write all this down (and then give parts of it away over the Internet). To my agents at the Kim Dawson Agency for keeping me working through several comebacks. And to Richard Feldman of the Julliard School for helping me to understand just how important concentration of attention is for the contemporary actor-in-training.

INTRODUCTION

This book will not teach you how to audition. You should already know how to do that before taking up the advanced practices detailed in this book. However, for convenience sake, the first chapter to follow will review, at a very high level, the basics of the process so at least we can agree on what you should already have mastered. This book's title is 150% *Better* Auditions, which implies from the start that you already understand the basics. My intention, as the author, is to help you *improve* upon what you are already (hopefully) pretty good at.

In order to make the best use of this book then, you should already know the basic process of auditioning, for stage and/or screen, depending on where you work in the industry. You should already know, for instance, to arrive 15 minutes early; always bring a head shot (even when not asked); look for the sign-in sheet first thing when you walk in the door; be polite to the casting assistants (all of them); don't talk too much (or too loudly) in the waiting area; know your lines (but still hold the script in your hand); don't be nervous; be funny, confident, and focused; listen to all instructions; take direction well (even when you don't agree with it); and make brilliant, strong choices even under the most artificial and distracting circumstance that could ever be conceived of for doing the kind of intimate, personal work expected of an auditioning actor. Easy, right?

Once you have mastered the sequence of events portrayed above, this book will help you *improve* upon those skills necessary to successfully navigate, and compete more effectively in, the absurd situation that we actors know as the audition process. So, in effect, this book is intended for those who have already gone "pro" or who are at the point of joining the professional ranks of actors that regularly compete for paying gigs in the vast entertainment industry, whether that is on- or off- Broadway, regional theatre, television commercials, voice overs, industrial/educational films, animation, episodic TV series, or major films.

If you are an inexperienced amateur, student, or beginner who is just starting out, this book may still be of value to you, but you may want to visit my website, www.KevinPage.com, for a list of references and resources on basic audition techniques that you should probably be familiar with if you hope to succeed as a professional actor. Once again, this book will help you get *better* at that; there are plenty of other places to learn the fundamentals.

Why should you listen to my advice about auditioning, acting, or anything else? Well, for one thing, I have been a successful working actor for over 30 years, since my first speaking role in a major feature film (I was killed by a robot in the 1987 classic, *RoboCop*). I have appeared in over 70 movies and TV episodes; had guest starring arcs on *Seinfeld* (NBC), *Wishbone* (PBS), and *Dallas* (the 2012-2014 reboot on TNT), where I played the character that finally shot and killed the iconic "JR Ewing" (played by the late, great Larry Hagman). I've played opposite dozens of stars, including Robert De Niro, Billy Bob Thornton, Linda Gray, Jerry Seinfeld, Jason Alexander, Susan Lucci, Dolph Lundgren, Chuck Norris, Jean Claude Van Damme, Carol O'Connor,

Scott Bakula, and Jeff Daniels, to name a few. I have done dozens of TV commercials, voice overs, and industrial films (mostly to pay the rent). And I have had to audition for *every one of those jobs*. But that's not why you should listen to my advice.

In addition to having studied acting at a major university conservatory in the 1980s (SMU's Meadow's School of the Arts MFA Acting Program), I also hold a Master's degree in psychology where I did original research on meditation and human consciousness. In grad school, I became fascinated by the similarities between meditation training and actor training and spent almost a decade working out a system for utilizing meditation practice as part of the actor training process. I have written two books on acting theory, both will be published in late 2018 by global publishing powerhouse, Routledge. This book, in part, is an adaptation of my actor-centric mindfulness meditation program I introduce in *Advanced Consciousness Training (A.C.T.) for Actors* (Page, 2018). However, that's not why you should listen to me either.

I am very *good* at auditioning and have been for a very long time. I decided early in my career, while I was still working on my MFA, that if I couldn't audition well, I wouldn't get the jobs I wanted, so I spent a lot of time working on that particular aspect of my craft. While most actors I knew at that time hated and feared walking into that audition room, I decided to try and love it, to make it my *favorite* part of being an actor instead of the part that made me cringe. I read a ton of very good books about how to audition for both stage and screen mediums (again, see my website for a list of basic references, www.KevinPage.com, under *Audition Basics Toolkit*), I took every opportunity to audition that I could get (just for the experience and to master my own fear), and eventually convinced myself I actually *liked* the audition process itself as a type of weird, uncertain kind of athletic challenge where the rules were always changing and the refs were not always fair, but at the same time anyone had a chance to win the game! Nonetheless, much like all actors, I still got nervous, distracted, and unnerved by the competition much of the time. Until, that is, I started applying the meditation (mindfulness) practices I had learned as part of my research on actor training and the audition process. And suddenly ... I got better! A lot better, even after 30 years as a professional. And *that's* why you should read this book and try for yourself what I am going to suggest to you as ways to improve yourself as both an actor and a human being.

This is not a how-to guide but a self-help book for actors that want to improve their craft and book more professional, paying gigs. In auditioning to get the job, there are three very important qualities that all good actors have naturally, to one degree or another: concentration, relaxation under pressure, and an ability to "be present in the moment" (and respond spontaneously to what they find there). I will be discussing all three of these qualities in the following chapters, but here is the basic fact that they almost never teach you in acting class or at the university theatre department: All three of these critical qualities *can be trained directly*. That's what this book will show you how to do. 1) To concentrate and focus your attention more fully. 2) To relax even in intensely awkward or artificial circumstances that conspire to blow your cool. 3) To be completely present in the moment without being distracted by the other actors or the crazy things that always get thrown at you inside the audition room. It is my contention that if you can improve those three qualities within yourself, the quality and consistency of your auditions will improve significantly, as much as 150%, guaranteed!

The subtitle of this book is "Using Mindfulness Practice to Improve Your Acting." That really gets to the heart of it. I will not try and teach you how to act or even how to audition. As I've already said, that is for you to do on your own and there are plenty of resources available to help you build those basic, prerequisite skills. The point of this book is to help actors improve *themselves* and, as a result of it, their ability to audition well. This is something that happened for me, and I will show you how I did it.

The marvelous thing about the techniques and exercises shared in the following pages is that you don't have to take my word for any of it. You can test these methods in your own experience and be the sole judge as to whether they help you or not. The only down side here is that, if you don't actually *do* the exercises, if you only read about them or think about doing them, you will receive no benefits whatsoever. In order to help yourself with what I will show you, you have to *practice the techniques over time*, not just entertain ideas about them.

So, this is my promise to you: If you actually *do* the work I introduce in this book, you will become better, *significantly better*, at both auditioning and acting across your entire professional career.

Enjoy what you learn here, and … break a leg!

1 AUDITION BASICS: WHAT YOU SHOULD ALREADY KNOW

So, you're an actor? You've taken classes, or maybe even gotten a BFA at your local university. You've invested in head shots. You've been in a dozen plays (some of them actually pretty good productions). You've finally landed an agent in whatever market you plan to work in. And you even have a nice "bite-and-smile" close-up in an upcoming cable commercial for a regional fast food restaurant. Congratulations! That's quite an accomplishment.

Perhaps you've progressed even farther than that. Maybe you have both your Equity (AEA) and SAG/AFTRA cards (that means you're in the unions, for those that don't know)? You've done a couple of good commercials and have even been called back for the occasional day-player role on a TV drama or sit-com. Again, that's fantastic!

One last scenario. You're an old hand, a seasoned performer with a resume full of co-star and guest shots on major shows and/or features. You're on your third agent in Hollywood, and even play poker some weekends with people that would have made you nervous when you were first starting out. You've made it. Your established. Bravo!

It's even possible that you're a student, just starting out, not even sure how an audition works much less ready to sit in a casting office with established stars to compete for a series regular on a hit cable show. That would be too scary to even contemplate for a couple of years until you've gotten your feet wet. No worries. Read on. There's something here for everyone.

In any of the cases above, at each level, you will all have at least one thing in common as actors: You will invariably have to audition to win your next role, pretty much regardless of how famous you get. That's just how show business works.

Here's another thing that most actors will have in common, regardless of their level of previous accomplishments. Almost universally, actors *hate* to audition! It's like some unspoken rule of the Universe. Why is that? Why do actors almost universally despise the one activity that can bring them work, income, and the respect of their peers and fans?

I think actors hate to audition for a couple of pretty tangible reasons. First, the audition process, whether for stage or screen, is almost always nerve-racking in one unexpected way or another. You haven't had enough time to prepare. The room is filled with competing actors, all of whom look like a slightly more handsome/pretty version of yourself, and all seem to have just a smidge more talent than you do (at least from where you sit, huddled in your corner of the waiting room). The casting assistant is a terrible reader and keeps stepping on your lines or not giving you enough time to react "organically." The director doesn't look up from her sandwich the entire time that you're in the room. The casting director "doesn't like you." The list of indignities related to the audition scenario appears to be endless.

The second prominent reason actors seem to hate to audition is the level of competition. Face it. If you are in a major market and auditioning for a major role of any kind (commercial, TV, feature film, et al) the casting department may initially interview or pre-read anywhere between 100 and 500 actors for a single role. So, the odds of success in any particular casting situation are really incredibly low. Again, that's just how show business works!

Those two general categories of difficulty/challenge tend to make actors not enjoy doing the one thing that they have to do in order to work: audition. This is unfortunate but also unavoidable. If you want to be an actor, particularly one that makes a living doing what you love, then you have to be able to audition well and often if you hope to succeed.

As I mentioned in the Introduction, I decided early on in my career to try to buck the crowd and learn to love the entire audition process. It wasn't easy, but over time, I was actually able to pull that off. I genuinely enjoy auditioning (usually) and have become very good at it over the years. In this chapter, I will share some of my own unique process and even a few tricks I have learned along the way. But, more important, in recent years I have found a new approach to auditioning, acting, and living the life of an actor that has helped me become even better at my craft, and that is what I will share in the later chapters of this book. It is what I call a self-help program for the actor that can help reduce nerves, increase the ever important quality of attentional focus, and generally help you find the calm in the middle of the "present moment" whether that moment is happening in an audition, on the stage, or in front of an entire bank of cameras recording every twitch or movement of your face and eyes. To me, that is the real value of the book you hold in your hand (or are reading from your computer screen).

In preparing to write this book, I read or reread the best books I could find on the audition process to see what others had offered as advice before me. And, it turns out, there's a lot of good advice already out there! That was how I figured out that my book didn't need to be a how-to manual so much as a how-to-do-better manual.

Let me start by laying out, in a general way, what other authors and teachers have said about learning to audition properly. This will be a synopsis. If you really want to learn these techniques from the ground up, you will need to read the original books. (A complete list of reference materials can be found on my website at: www.KevinPage.com, under *Audition Basics Toolkit*.) But for now, let this serve as a refresher course.

Audition Basics—Books

One of the best books on the process of auditioning that I have ever read is *Auditioning: An Actor-friendly Guide* by Joanna Merlin (2001). Merlin, who is an actor as well as a casting director herself, has written a heart-felt, sensitive, and deeply insightful book on the actor's role in the audition process, whether that audition is for stage, screen, or "other." She captures the feelings, emotions, and self-judgments that almost always go along with auditioning under pressure and puts the whole experience into the context of a complete production (including the casting department, director, production crew, and other actors vying for your same role.) If nothing else, her book will make you feel better about yourself for joining the circus that is most often the acting profession. *Auditioning* is a must read for every actor, beginner-through-star.

Another classic book on the audition process is entitled simply *Audition: Everything an Actor Needs to Know to Get the Part* by Michael Shurtleff (1978). Shurtleff has basically written an acting book (and a very good one) that, while ostensibly aimed at the audition experience, is really more of a general explication of being present and connected to the moment of performance. Some of the text is a bit dated, and its narrative is mostly aimed at auditioning for the theatre, but it remains a classic acting book that probably should be read by every actor as part of their basic training.

The Art of Auditioning: Techniques for Television by Rob Decina (2004) is a detailed system for auditioning for television (heavily weighted toward daytime drama—soap operas—which is a mostly dead form at this point in history) from the perspective of a casting director. Decina offers a number of specific pointers that can give the actor comfort in understanding the technical aspects of a camera audition along with a practical narrative about acting during the artificial circumstances surrounding most audition scenarios. Again, some of the information is dated, but if you are just learning about the audition process, Decina's book offers another distinct perspective that can be quite useful.

Auditioning and Acting for the Camera by John W. Shepard (2004) offers the perspective of a long-time actor, as well as acting teacher, on the art of presenting yourself on camera for auditions in several common genres, including film, episodic TV, sitcoms, soap operas, commercials, industrials, and on location. Separating out "on location" as a stand-alone genre of performance at first may seem like an odd choice until you realize that Shepard explains a good deal of technical and practical aspects of filming on location that are generally not shared in a typical auditioning book. In addition to offering auditioning advice, Shepard shares a great number of technical aspects of the business that are very useful to know in advance of actually working on a set, particularly if you are a beginner and have never worked in any of these genres before.

A couple of more recent examples of basic audition technique books that focus specifically on camera acting in various genres are *Auditioning on Camera: An Actor's Guide* (Hacker, 2012), and *Auditioning for Commercials: What to Expect* (Holdren, 2016). Both of these books offer industry-specific advice and a lot of technical detail that can prepare you for the practical aspects of auditioning for film, television, and commercials (which are a very specific genre in their own right).

By reading several books on the basics of the professional audition situation, you can feel confident when you show up at the theatre or casting office that you know what to expect. Below, I will summarize a number of the key points touched on in most of these books that can serve as a checklist of things you should know or consider before making yourself available, on a professional basis, to audition for paid acting gigs.

Technical Elements of an Audition

A professional actor must eventually become comfortable with ambiguity and uncertainty. You will simply never be absolutely certain of what is going to happen in the audition room and so must be ready for anything and able to take whatever happens in stride. Interestingly, the practice of meditation (which we will discuss in the second half of this book) has been shown to help cultivate this quality.

Here is a list of the most basic possibilities and technical elements that you are most likely to confront. However, they will rarely be the same elements, in the same combination, from situation to situation, which is why it is important to be familiar with the following but not rigidly dependent on them. You're an actor, one of your main jobs is to stay cool under pressure.

- You will receive a call from your agent (or identify the opportunity through some other source) with an appointment time to read for a particular role

- The initial information you receive should include the character's name or other identifier ("business man #1," "girl behind the counter," "Cop #2") and a character description (often called a "breakdown"), as well as a brief description of the show or commercial. The amount and specificity of this information will vary, but make sure to carefully read and consider ALL information you receive. Other than the portion of the script you will be reading, this is all you will have to go on before your initial reading

- The initial information may also include items such as potential shoot/production dates (make sure to check your calendar for possible conflicts and be ready to report them to your agent or at the audition itself).

- In addition to a character description, you will receive a small portion of a script (called "sides") containing between one and three scenes of dialogue (if it is a speaking role). Learn this dialogue thoroughly, but plan on holding the sides in your hand during your audition. This serves two purposes. First, if you forget a line, you can simply glance down, find your place, and move on with the scene as if nothing had happened. Second, holding the sides reminds everyone that it is an audition and not a polished performance.

- When you leave your house or apartment for your appointment, make sure you have everything you are going to need. This will include a head shot with résumé stapled to the back, your sides or commercial copy (even if you already have it memorized), costume pieces or changes of clothes you may need for the actual audition, combs, brushes, hairspray, or additional makeup for touchups before you go into the audition room.

- Make sure you arrive at the audition location at least 15 minutes early (you don't have to enter the actual room until 5-10 minutes ahead of your appointed time, but you will want to make sure you have located the entrance to the office well in advance of your appointment).

- When you enter the audition waiting area, you will find a sign-in sheet. Make sure to fill out the required information. If it is a union job, the form may ask for your Social Security number. Many actors (including myself) are uncomfortable writing down this information on a sheet that everyone has access to. It is acceptable to write "upon hire" into this section.

- In most cases, there will be other actors waiting to go into the audition room. These actors may or may not be reading for the same role as you. Do not let this throw you or affect your confidence; you are there to do your best job, not judge the competition. Seeing the competition often makes actors nervous. Instead, resist this impulse and concentrate on reading over your sides and otherwise holding your concentration on *your* audition. Focusing on your sides is an effective way to "tune out distractions" while you wait your turn and also to avoid unnecessary conversation while in the waiting area. (If you get caught up into a loud social conversation in the waiting room, you may disrupt the people inside the audition and get yourself into trouble; there are few things less professional than interrupting someone else's audition.)

- When you are called into the formal audition space, which can be a stage (for theatre), video studio, office, or hotel room, make sure you are carrying your sides and headshot in your hand (unless you have been told specifically that you won't need a head shot). Hand your head shot to the casting assistant or director. Do not try to shake the director's or casting director's hand unless they offer their hand first. And make sure to smile and be friendly for your first impression.

- If it is an on-camera audition, you may be asked to "slate" for the camera before (or after) you begin. Usually, they will tell you what they want to hear in your slate. The basic slate consists of looking directly into the camera, stating your name, your agency (if any) and the name of the character you are reading for. Again, there can be variations on this, so listen carefully to any instructions before you start. The casting assistant will roll the video camera and cue you with an "action" (or similar phrase) before you slate.

- After your slate (if there is one), you will read your scene with the casting director or a casting assistant. Focus your attention, as appropriate, on the person you are reading with and proceed to read whatever scenes you were provided.

- Remember that your audition actually begins when you enter the audition space and doesn't end until you leave the office or theatre. Everything you do from the time the camera rolls until it is turned off will be recorded, so be aware that what you do between scenes or even before you start is part of your audition. Because how you behave before the scene or in between scenes can be just as interesting (and informative) about you as an actor and a professional, stay focused and intense the whole time you are in the room. That doesn't mean you can't be friendly if the director wants to chat, but it does mean to "stay real" and purposeful while that camera is rolling or you are standing at center stage.

- If the director or casting director gives you notes or instructions and asks you to do the scene again, do your best to incorporate those notes or instruction into your performance. This is a test to see how well you take direction and it is highly important that you pay careful attention to these instructions.

- Under no circumstances, even if you have flubbed a

line or made a foolish mistake, are you to indicate your own disappointment or self-judgment while you are in the audition room. Do not ask to start again or "can I do that over." Simply move forward with the scene and get back to where you need to be as if nothing had happened. This is important because, self-deprecation is not attractive or useful for actors. Furthermore, actors who can demonstrate their ability to "stay with" a scene are also demonstrating an ability to concentrate their attention and to think on their feet, two very important qualities for a professional actor to have. You can win a role by demonstrating your ability to operate under pressure and to solve unexpected problems much faster than you will win a role by showing embarrassment and apologizing for yourself. In fact, many small mistakes that loom large in an actor's consciousness may go completely unnoticed by the director if the focus of the performer stays on the scene.

- When the audition is over, don't linger and make small-talk (unless asked), thank the people in the room, and leave.

- Take a few moments to sign out on the sign-in sheet (there will usually be a spot for your initials) and gather any items you left in the lobby. Do not simply bolt out the door. This brief interlude before you leave the audition office actually serves a purpose. Sometimes, in the moments after you leave the audition room, the director or casting director may decide that they want you to read a different role. They may come out up to two or three minutes after you leave the room and ask you to stay for further reading. Once the next person has gone in, you are free to exit the room and go home.

- Do not have loud conversations about how it went or

anything else regarding the audition at the audition location or even in the parking lot. I like to say that the audition begins when you get out of the car (or leave your apartment) and ends when you are back in your car (or apartment). Anything that happens between those two locations can be overheard by others and, therefore, can play some (possibly negative) role in your either getting hired or making an impression that will be remembered.

Having read the books on audition basics and armed with the above list of technical guidelines, you will be prepared for most any situation. In the meantime, keep taking acting classes with the best teachers you can access and working with the best people you can to hone your acting skills. As Joanna Merlin says in her book, *Auditioning: An Actor-Friendly Guide*, "losing [a role] because of your own lack of preparedness is a poor alternative" (p. 9).

There is one other technical scenario that has become a possibility only in the last couple of years—self-taping. Self-taping can be accomplished one of two ways: either hire a freelance taping studio or literally tape yourself using a video camera or even your smart phone. The important things to remember when self-taping are that you need to make the tape look just as good as those that are shot in the casting session or at a professional casting studio and that *your performance needs to be just as compelling as if you had given it in the room in front of the director*. The good news is that with a self-taped audition, you control all of the normally uncontrollable parameters, meaning you get multiple takes to get it "just right" and there should be no one else around to distract you. The not-so-good news is that you need to have access to enough technology and a mastery of that technology to be able to reliably produce a quality tape on your own or have the money to pay someone who does. In acting, everything has its tradeoffs. In either case, the same three issues/qualities discussed in the next section will apply.

Is an Audition Acting?

Each of the authors of the books I mentioned earlier have a slightly different take on whether or not an audition is the same thing as acting. For instance, casting director Rob Decina firmly believes that auditioning is *not* acting, per se, and needs to be looked at in a different light than performance. Whereas, Joanna Merlin believes that the audition circumstance is "an opportunity to reveal your ability to play a particular role" (p. 14). I think of an audition as a full-blown performance, with certain restrictions and parameters that are forced upon it by the circumstances (which are ever changing). Even though it is different from being on a film set or a live stage performance with an audience, I still give the same all-out level of performance that I would "on the day," but I tailor that performance to the demands of the room instead of the finished film or stage play.

Once you realize that as a professional actor you will audition significantly more times than you actually perform on stage or on screen, it becomes obvious that the majority of the actor's performance opportunities will be spent auditioning (or you won't work in the other formats very much at all). Those are the facts of the actor's life. So, literally, if you enjoy being an actor, by default, you *must* enjoy auditioning. If that seems like a strange truth to swallow, read on because I have several non-ordinary ways to approach this fact-of-the-business that can actually "flip the script" on your attitude towards auditioning and even make the whole process sort of fun (and wouldn't that be a huge advantage over your competition?).

In any event, whether or not you believe that an audition is a "real" performance, you need to be as prepared as possible for the unpredictable events you will undoubtedly confront when the time comes.

So, how does one prepare for something as unpredictable as the audition situation?

The Three Keys to Successful Auditioning (Under Any Circumstance)

I believe there are three basic qualities possessed by actors (all of which can be trained) that directly affect their ability to meet any situation and deliver their very best work regardless of the circumstances. These are:

- Concentration (the ability to focus attention)

- Relaxation (particularly under pressure)

- Presence in the moment (and reacting spontaneously to what you find there)

For my book, *Advanced Consciousness Training (A.C.T.) for Actors* (2018), I interviewed more than 20 top acting teachers at famous acting conservatories around the world, including Richard Feldman (Julliard), Walton Wilson (Yale School of Drama), and Lucy Skilbeck (Royal Academy of Dramatic Arts), and they all agreed that the abilities to concentrate attention, remain relaxed, and "live fully in the moment" were qualities of the highest importance to the successful actor. I also believe this to be true and that is why I identify these three qualities as *the most important*, not only to acting in performance but to acting in the audition room. The rest of this book will be dedicated to cultivating and perfecting these three qualities that have the power to significantly improve your auditioning success.

As I said before, this is a self-help book for professional actors. Only, instead of helping you get over your problems, I'm going to help you get better at what you already know how to do. This book gives you tools to develop your existing talents, skills, and potentials to their highest possible degree.

In the following chapters we will be looking at techniques and practices that research tells us can help the individual more fully focus their attention at will, cultivate a deep physical and mental relaxation that can be carried into any situation, and become (and stay) fully present in the "now" moment where great auditions always happen. These techniques are rarely offered in acting classes or "how to" audition courses. Some of what I will share is based on ancient meditation practices developed over centuries. Some is adapted from scientific studies conducted over the past 20 years that have identified ways to purposefully change brain chemistry and states of consciousness. In all cases, what I offer in the following pages has been tried by me in the field and I attest to the effectiveness and potential of these techniques, when properly applied, to transform what you do as an actor and the results you achieve in the audition room.

2 WHAT GETS IN YOUR WAY

Most actors think of themselves as psychologists in one form or another. They make decisions about characters, how they feel, how they might react under certain circumstances, and such. But interestingly enough, very few actors actually spend much time studying psychology or what the various schools of psychological thought have to say about human behavior and experience.

One of the more powerful insights of contemporary psychology has to do with how our brains react to certain external situations, like stress or uncertainty. Interestingly, there has been a lot of recent research performed by psychologists on the very kinds of situations that actors go through on a daily basis. And the results of that research are pretty conclusive. Stress, distraction, negative self-talk, all have a negative effect on brain chemistry and, furthermore, these negative effects can be counteracted by certain kinds of exercises (things like meditation and mindfulness practice) if applied in a conscious, sustained fashion. In other words, science has discovered what the ancient yogis and Zen masters have known for centuries: You can rewire your own brain to be more focused, less nervous, and more present—the exact qualities we identified in the last chapter as being most important for success to the actor!

So, what gets in your way when you head out for an audition and how can you remove those obstacles? Interestingly, the top three impediments to a superb audition experience are the opposites of the three most important qualities: 1) distraction and scattered attention, 2) nervousness and insecurities, and 3) thinking about the past or future instead of being present in the moment. Let's take each one of these separately.

The Distracted Actor

Distracted or disorganized thinking, particularly as a result of overusing digital devices, has become epidemic in the developed world. When I was interviewing some of the top master acting teachers in the world for my upcoming book, I was surprised at how often this topic came up. Even at top conservatories, like Yale, Julliard, NYU, and many others, young actors have become so distracted by chronic cellphone use and multitasking that many teachers collect mobile phones at the beginning of class. I was even told that student actors are not getting to know their classmates as well (a critical part of building a strong acting ensemble) because they are on their phones between classes instead of talking to each other.

For an excellent book on the overall effects of digital distraction on individuals and society, see *The Distracted Mind: Ancient Brains in a High-tech World* by Gazzaley and Rosen (2016).

This pervasive distraction is particularly important to actors today because the deployment and focus of attention is considered to be the actor's most valuable asset. When you go on stage or step in front of a camera, you take nothing with you but your focus of attention; rehearsal is in the past, and so is your training. When you act, there is *only* attention. The actor must have an extraordinary ability to focus and attend to the tasks required by the scene. Superb attentional control is not a "nice to have," it is a requirement for success in show business. Period.

If you find yourself multitasking regularly, checking your cellphone more than once an hour, using social media as a way to avoid in-person contact, etc., you may be damaging your ability to concentrate and focus your attention at will. If you are interested in the research behind this, see my book *Advanced Consciousness Training (A.C.T.) for Actors* coming out in September of 2018 from Routledge Press. In it, you will find a detailed conversation on this topic and a number of things you can do to counteract it.

The good news is that there are a number of very practical ways you can train your attentional focus, which I will share in the chapters that follow. At the most basic level: better concentration of attention (less distraction) = better auditions.

The Nervous or Insecure Actor

Nerves and insecurity have plagued actors since the beginning of the art in prehistoric times. And nervousness in the artificial and extra-intense context of an audition situation is particularly deadly. If your hands are shaking, you're dripping sweat down your forehead into your eyes, and your voice is quivering while you are trying to be commanding, confident, or sexy … you will probably not get the job or even a callback. Those are simply the facts of the business. Confidence and a self-assured attitude are absolute requirements for success at an audition and in the business as a whole. After all, if acting makes you feel bad, why are you doing it in the first place?

There are a thousand different causes of anxiety before, during, and after an audition. You're running late and are feeling under-prepared; the room is filled with other actors that look just like you (several of whom have beat you out for roles in the past); the casting director seems unfriendly or doesn't read the dialogue like you had planned, to name a few. And simply telling yourself "don't be nervous" under such circumstances is probably not of much help either. However, as with the concentration of attention discussed above, there are ways of training yourself to reduce nervousness and reverse insecurity.

Most nervousness and insecurity are caused by an attachment to outcomes. If you weren't worried about getting the job, impressing the director, or making the money you need to pay rent, you probably wouldn't be nervous at all. If you already had the job and were just reading the scenes with other actors to help them get cast, you would probably enjoy the audition situation! This book can help you with that. Mindfulness practice, introduced in the next chapter, has been shown by research to reduce stress (even the physical symptoms like shaky hands or sweaty palms) and the attachment to outcomes, creating what is often called a sense of equanimity. Dictionary.com defines equanimity as "mental calmness, composure, and evenness of temper, especially in a difficult situation." Doesn't that sound like a useful state to be able to consciously cultivate right before an audition? Read on …

The Actor Living in the Past/Future

Not being present to what is happening in the audition room will almost always ruin your chances of giving a superb audition, no matter how well prepared you might have been before entering the room. In an audition, you are being asked to respond to several things spontaneously all at once. You need to be warm and friendly to the directors, producers, and assistants in the room; you need to hit your mark and take direction; you may need to slate your name and agent for the camera before you start right into a heavy emotional scene. And if you are distracted by what happened just before you walked into the room, or if you are thrown off by what has been asked of you, or if you are thinking more about getting the job than actually listening to the direction, you will not be in the present moment and deliver your best work when the casting director calls, "Action!"

Once again, research has shown that the practices described in this book can actually help you stay in the present moment as an act of will. After all, as you will see below, mindfulness meditation practice is literally all about being (and staying) in the present.

Unfortunately, very little of what is taught in traditional acting classes helps you deal with these three issues directly. I strongly believe that a mindfulness practice, such as the one proposed in this book, should be included in every actor's basic training regimen. However, you can be the judge of that yourself, as what this book requires is that you actually do the mindfulness practices, not just read about them. So, once you have completed the training program outlined below, you will be able to judge by your own experience how useful it is to be less distracted, more confident, and supremely awake in the present moment when you walk into the audition room.

Who Takes a Cat to a Football Game?

Imagine that you take your favorite cat to a professional football game. You love this cat so much that you have purchased her the seat right next to yours so she will have a nice place of her own to curl up during the game (if you are not a cat lover, just go along with the scenario for the time being).

It is the fourth quarter and the home team has just scored a big touchdown. As the fans roar, you jump to your feet along with the rest of the crowd and cheer your approval.

Question: Can you hear the cat purring as she sleeps through the cacophony of noise? Of course not! There is way too much sensory input to allow you to pick up on the subtle purring sound of the sleeping cat. Your attention is inevitably drawn to, and your senses overwhelmed by, the noise and excitement going on all around you. This is essentially how the untrained mind is all the time, continually lost in the excitement of ongoing experience like a spectator at the football game of life!

Now, let's imagine the game is over (and your team won) and you are back in your car preparing to drive home. Can you hear the cat now? Perhaps. It depends on the number of distractions you are faced with while driving through the heavy, post-game traffic. You might well be able to hear the cat purr, but more likely you will be focused on the road in front of you, the pedestrians making their way to their cars, the signals of police directing traffic, etc. In other words, while the inside of your car is relatively less noisy than the football stadium after a touchdown, there is still a lot of input to distract you from the cat.

Finally, you are home. You sit in your favorite chair, a glass of wine in your hand, and the cat jumps into your lap for a nap. In the silence of your own home, with the doors closed and the window shades drawn, it is easy to hear the gentle, rhythmic purring of the cat in your lap.

That is how mindfulness training works. It stills the mind, allowing you to shut out distractions and sense the subtle, moment-to-moment sensations of just being present to the happenings of the moment, in this case, sitting in a chair listening to your favorite cat purring.

Being able to control your attention, how it is deployed and directed, is an absolutely critical ability for the actor to develop. Here is an example.

An earlier generation of actors, which included Robert De Niro, Meryl Streep, Al Pacino, Glenn Close, Gene Hackman, and many others, were all known for the intensity of their stage and film performances. I argue that these actors' intensity was not a product of their training, technique, or self-discipline gained over the years, for certainly they had all of these as prerequisites, as much as it was a product of their individual abilities to focus their attention at will during a performance. After all, while they may have had years of training behind them, when they stepped on stage or in front of the camera, that training could not go with them: It was in the past.

What each of those actors brought into the moment of performance was a hyper-focused quality of attention that channeled their personal intensity to their audience. *They were listening to the cat!* That's the quality that the exercises in this book will help you develop.

3 INTERLUDE ONE: A DAY IN THE LIFE OF AN ACTOR

A Typical Day in the Life of an Auditioning Actor

The following story illustrates the types of stresses that can distract you, undermine your confidence, and affect your concentration of attention in the present moment. This example is taken from actual events, although some of the details have been changed because of non-disclosure agreements (now common when you audition for series television jobs). If you are new to the life of professional acting, consider this a "typical day at the office." If you are already a pro, you will recognize this as a generic example of the kinds of challenges you meet every day.

Late on a Monday afternoon, while I was sitting at my computer writing this book, I received an email from my agent about a commercial audition that I was called for that was to take place on Wednesday in another city. If I wanted to do the reading, I would have to travel approximately 180 miles (3 hours by car) or fly, which was going to cost over $500 (not to mention the cab and Uber fees I would rack up driving around the city to make my appointment). So, my first challenge was deciding whether to invest a large amount of money or spend over 6 hours negotiating dangerous highways just to get to the reading.

This particular audition was for a series of local ads that was supposed to shoot over the next 3 years and, therefore, would be potentially *very* lucrative for whoever was selected as the spokesman. (Between 45 and 90 individual session fees plus radio and internet usage, even for a local ad series, can equal a six-figure income!) I decided to make the investment in a plane ticket and preserve my energy instead of making a draining 3-hour road trip right before my reading. The one-hour flight would leave at noon, giving me plenty of time to make it to the office where I was scheduled to read at 3:20 p.m. I had a return flight at 5:15 p.m, which was tight but reasonable given the casting location.

I started working on memorizing the commercial copy, which was traditional spokesperson language for a law firm: wordy, confident jargon. I checked my personal grooming (nails trimmed, hair length appropriate, etc.) and made sure that my most conservative blue suit was clean and pressed. I often wear a 2-3 day beard in case I get a film or TV audition that wants a more rugged look. I am blessed to be one of those actors who can believably play a tough guy on a TV drama and if you clean me up, I can also be a spokesman or friendly "dad type" for commercial work. I made a note that I would need to have a good shave before I caught my flight in a little under 36 hours.

The next morning, at 10:30 a.m., I received a new email from my agent. I had been invited to audition for a major TV series that was shooting on location in the city that I was flying to the next day. They wanted me to read for two different parts; one was a guest starring role, the other a recurring character that could potentially go on for the entire season. The show was a historical drama set in the old West, and the recurring role was a down-on-his-luck ranch hand (definitely requiring my 2-3 day beard!). The other role was a well-dressed businessman (where the suit from the commercial audition would be appropriate attire.) I realized that, if I were lucky, I could do both auditions on the same day. Suddenly, my investment in airline tickets was looking more justified as I now had three important auditions instead of one!

The call time was flexible, so I requested an earlier time slot for the TV series so that I could keep my beard, do the series audition, shave, change into my suit, and still have enough time to Uber to the location for the commercial audition some 5 miles away. However, it turned out that the TV series casting director only had time slots available between 4:00 p.m. and 5:00 p.m. for the roles I was to read for. Dilemma. This meant, at a minimum, that I would have to go to the commercial audition first (clean shaven and in a suit), then travel across town at rush hour, still in my suit for the first role and then costume change for the more important recurring role. But, I would only have, at a maximum, one hour to make it there—a high-risk proposition in a town known for its daily traffic jams.

To try and make this all work, I asked my agent to accept the 4:00-5:00 p.m. TV audition time and contact the producers of the commercial to see if they would see me an hour earlier, which they agreed to. I then had to change my return flight from 5:15 p.m. to 8:30 p.m. so that I could get home and not have to pay for a hotel room as well. Luckily, the later commuter flight was available. At this point, I could have chosen to drive; however, now in addition to all the wordy commercial copy I had to learn, I had eight pages of fairly difficult dialogue to memorize in a little more than a day. Add to that, the series I was reading for was going into its second season and while I had heard of it before, I had never watched it. The cast included some major stars (some of which I would be working with if I won the gig), and the first season had just become available for streaming. I therefore decided to watch as much of the show as I could before traveling the next day. At this point, I had just 26 hours before I was scheduled to read for the show. I started watching the series from the pilot episode, where the main characters were introduced, and managed to get through 7 of the 10 episodes (including the season finale) before going to bed that night. But I still did not have all of my lines memorized. That would take most of the rest of my travel day, so to drive instead of fly would now have been impossible.

Is this giving you a sense for how fast-paced (and potentially stressful) professional auditioning can be? Remember, all of the dialogue, which I had to learn to perfection, came to me through email with only a day to a day and a half to memorize it all. Plus, the spokesman role and acting scenes were all difficult, complex technical achievements to play in a believable manner (not to mention they were three very *different* kinds of roles!). This is why I am not attempting to teach you how to audition; that is something that, in most cases, takes years to learn and master. However, in order to deliver a performance-ready audition under the kinds of circumstances I am describing, the actor needs to stay cool, calm, and collected under pressure, which is at least as important as technique when you are actually *in* the situation.

The story continues. At 5:15 p.m. on the evening before I was to attempt all three of these audition challenges, I received another email from my agent. I had been requested for the following morning at 11:20 a.m. (40 minutes before my flight was to take off) to read for yet another commercial at a local casting office in town, which is located (luckily) just 15 minutes from the airport. By looking at what times other actors from my agency had been called for, I was able to deduce that the casting sessions began at 10:00 a. m. I immediately emailed my agent and told her to check with the casting director to see if they would be willing to take me in their first slot of the morning so that I could still make my flight. However, as it was well after business hours at this point, it was clear that I would not have a firm answer until the morning, with only a couple of hours to spare.

So here's the thing. At this point, I was only half through with my research for the TV series and it was important for me to understand the characters I would be asked to interact with if I hoped to land this kind of recurring character role. I had not yet had time to learn the lines, as I was busy watching the show, and had planned to do that in the morning before and while I was traveling. Now, I had a new piece of commercial copy I would have to learn by 10:00 a.m. the next morning (and I didn't even know yet if casting would approve the time change!). In order to pull all of this off, I needed to complete my research by bedtime, get up no later than 6:00 a.m. the next morning, learn the new commercial copy, drive to the audition (luckily, the role was a college basketball coach, so the suit and tie wardrobe I would already be in was acceptable), and get done in time to drive to the airport and make my 12:00 noon flight. If I had elected to drive to the other city, I would have had to pass on this fourth opportunity.

One final catch (this will be familiar to anyone who works regularly in commercials): The copy I received at 5:15 p.m. in the evening for an audition that was now (hopefully) scheduled at 10:00 a.m. the next morning (a short 16-hour time window) was *insanely* hard! It included lines with highly complex, technical terms that needed to be clearly articulated and precise, *and* performed at a high speed, trippingly off of the tongue, while acting out a comically emotional scene.

Now, try to imagine that you are a college basketball coach and it's the final moments of the championship game. Your best player has just been injured and you are huddled up with the remaining players, giving them a classic motivational speech on the sidelines before the last play (think of movies like *Hoosiers* or *Rudy*). In commercials, you are often asked to preform scenes that are essentially parodies of classic cinema or TV moments for comic effect. This was one of those moments. The speech I had to memorize (starting at 6:00 a.m. the next morning, giving me only 4 hours to do so in addition to packing, dressing for travel, and getting to the casting studio) went something like this:

"Okay. This is it! Your entire college careers are down to this moment. ... If you fail, we all go home losers. And you guys aren't losers!

"Baker and Hughes, you take the left. Blankenship and Carter, go right. Don't let their defense slow you down. And Frankenmuelar, you go straight up the middle. You understand?" (The camera pulls back to reveal a bright red pick-up truck in the center of the basketball court.)

"And remember, fellas, the new Excelsior pick-up truck has four-wheel drive, extensor-steering technology, and M-X5 hydro-flexor cruise control for a smoother driving experience that lets your family feel both safe and comfortable on the road at ALL times. (One of the players speaks; it's Frankenmuelar.)

"But Coach! What about accessories?"

"Don't worry about accessories, Frankenmuelar. The Excelsior is packed to the brim with digital climate controls, heated leather seats, and even a built-in entertainment center for kids! Now get out there and DRIVE THAT EXCELSIOR! (The crowd cheers as the team out maneuvers the other players on the court, jumps into the truck and peals out of the basketball court, the winners of the contest.)

Now try to imagine learning those lines so you can say them like an impassioned basketball coach in the heat of the moment. If you look down at the script, even once, it will throw off the rhythm of the scene and you will *not* get the job. Welcome to commercial acting!

I dutifully got up at 6:00 a.m., did my morning

meditation practice so I could start with a clear and steady mind, and started to work. At 7:08 a.m., I got the email from my agent: I was rescheduled for 10:00 a.m. for the truck audition. I would be able to make all 4 calls in the same day, 3 of them in a different city, before flying home that night after a 16-hour day.

How did it all turn out?

The first reading went pretty well. I just barely got the longer speeches about the truck accessories in my head (commercial clients tend to be very particular about exact wording, so there's no improvising there!) when they called me into the room with the director and someone from the ad agency. They seemed to like what I did, gave me some minor adjustments and asked me to do it a second time, "a little faster but with the same intensity." I happily obliged, following their instructions and delivering my lines at a brisker pace and with some other slight variations in my performance … until the last line. When I got to the last three words (which happened to be the tag-line for the entire product line: *DRIVE THAT EXCELSIOR!*), I said instead: "*DRIVE THAT EXCALIBER!*" At a commercial audition, to mispronounce the product's name (particularly in the all-important tag-line) is the kiss of death. I had blown it! Even though everyone in the room laughed and were polite, I knew that I would not get that job.

I thanked everyone in the room (trying to hide the embarrassment of my unforgivable line flub) and was off to the airport. I found parking with an hour to spare before my flight, changed my shirt, and put on a tie for the spokesman read, which was next on my list. The airport security line was long and slow, but I made it through with enough time to grab a sandwich before boarding my flight.

During the flight, which was only an hour long, I took a little more time to meditate as well as work on my lines for the next commercial audition. The copy for the spokesman gig was easier than the truck audition, but still required full attention to get memorized. Being a spokesman requires another set of specialty skills that must be learned and practiced over time. By the time I landed, I had my lines down cold—at least I thought I had.

I Ubered from the airport to the small office complex where the commercial company had rented a small suite to hold the auditions. The waiting area was maybe 10' x 15' and the casting assistant sat at a small table at one end of the room, signing people in on the union timesheet. There were maybe six chairs around the perimeter walls and four other actors (all in blue suits just like mine) standing around, mumbling the lines to themselves, some talking with each other while others walked in small circles, trying to memorize the sides.

Until you've had the chance to do this a few times, you should not underestimate how intimidating it is to walk into a room with a bunch of your competitors standing around looking and sounding a whole lot like you do! The way I deal with this is to be friendly and personable, particularly to the assistant who signs me in, but then mostly I look down at my script, continuing to practice silently until just before I am invited into the audition room. Some people may find me rude because I consciously avoid long conversations (that can be distracting), but mostly professionals understand this level of commitment and will leave you alone if they can see you are working. (I will sometimes also steal a few moments of calming meditation, but cover this by pretending to look at my script while I do so.)

As I said before, I thought I had my lines down well before I was called in. The audition parameters were fairly simple: Step on a mark on the floor, look straight into the camera, say your name when they give you the cue that the camera is rolling, and deliver the tough, calm, and confident speech directly into the camera lens like you were speaking to beloved family members or an intimate group of close friends.

The director, who was the only other person in the room besides the camera operator, made a few general comments about the style he was looking for before the camera rolled and I delivered my first take. Much to my horror, I got about halfway through this 30-second monologue and went completely blank on my next line. There was a long, awkward pause, while I looked down at the script in my hand and found my place, then looked up at the camera and continued on as if nothing had happened (even though my insides were crawling).

As I said before, commercial clients expect extreme accuracy in their language and the pace and flow with which it is delivered. That is what they are hiring you for and they expect to see it during the audition, or there is very little chance you will be hired. With film and TV, there is often more leeway with the lines as long as you deliver a believable performance, but not with commercials. I figured I was dead in the water. Somewhat to my surprise, because this is rarely the case, the director gave me a second take. He was friendly, told me to turn up the intensity a little more, and we did it again ... and I flubbed the line *again*! This time turning the last sentence into some kind of gibberish statement that made no sense.

When I was a less experienced actor, I would have been totally thrown off at this point and probably made a number of apologies to the director. However, if you are a pro, as most directors are, you know that people flub lines from time to time, so there is very little value in apologizing or making excuses. Instead, I chose to make a joke and let it go. Amazingly, the director gave me a third chance ... and I blew that one too! The lines simply would not come with an easy flow and I garbled their meaning yet again. He said "thank you." Then I said "thank you" and left the room with a smile and a wave, knowing full well that I did not get that job.

The lesson here is that sometimes, no matter how skilled or prepared you are, it just doesn't work out: You blow it. You don't have the great audition you know you are capable of. It is at times like these that the temptation to indulge in self-recriminations or negative self-talk can be strong. And, I admit, I knew I had blown it and I felt bad (after all, I had just spent over $600 dollars on plane tickets and cab fares to be there). But, I had two more readings scheduled that were also important, and I needed my head in the game because with only two hours left before those auditions, I still did not fully have my lines down! I generally knew the emotional tone and the beats of the scenes I was to read, but I needed more time to get the words to flow.

I called an Uber, put the last episode behind me, and started to work on the lines for my next reading. As it turned out, I still had a couple of hours to spend, so I had my ride drop me at a restaurant that was near the casting offices to grab a late lunch while I studied. I know from experience that it is a major mistake to go to an important audition on an empty stomach (you need the carbohydrate energy for the intensity required for most theatrical readings), so I was grateful to be able to grab a sandwich while I finished memorizing the sides.

At this point in my story, I have not said much about the role that my own mental state played in this series of events. Perhaps it's time for a bit of a testimonial.

Before I started using the techniques described in this book, I would have been far more nervous, stressed out, shaky, distracted, and demoralized after so much effort and clearly having failed my shot at a $100,000 job. In fact, even though the situation had been intense and filled with activity from the initial email on Monday up until this moment, I was able to handle it all with very few butterflies in the stomach. I used to sweat a lot when I would get nervous, but not anymore. It is still difficult to walk into a room of my long-time competitors and keep my focus, but I nonetheless stayed calm and confident (even sneaking in a couple of "conscious breaths" before going into the room—which I will explain in a later chapter). Most important, even though I had just suffered a major disappointment (as well as a blow to my ego), I was able to immediately shift gears and get my head back in the game for the next challenge. Without the attentional training I had been through, I might have kept going but I definitely would have been an emotional wreck!

When I got to the audition studio for my last two readings of the day, I was once again confronted with a room full of formidable-looking competitors, many of whom I had either worked with or auditioned against many times in the past. Once again, I signed in and buried my face in the first set of sides I was scheduled to read, not talking much with the other actors but concentrating on learning my lines and maintaining a high level of focus. Remember, I had been busy with commercial auditions prior to this, so when I arrived for this one, I still did not have my lines fully memorized. This is where the ability to focus your attention at will is invaluable—within 30 minutes, surrounded by other actors, many of whom were carrying on jocular social conversations, I was able to get the lines and the shape of the scene firmly in my head.

It was almost an hour before I was called in to read. You may recall that I was reading for a well-dressed businessman and so was still in the same suit and tie I started the day in. When I was called into the casting room I was greeted warmly by a casting director I had known for years and who had gotten me several jobs in the past.

The reading went well. This time I didn't flub any lines and was at the top of my game. We went through it twice, and the second time I really "nailed it," according to the casting director. She was pleased and so was I. I left the room, walked directly to the bathroom and changed from my suit into a flannel shirt and blue jeans, my "down-on-his-luck ranch hand" wardrobe.

When I returned to the audition holding area, where several of the other actors were milling around, I had not only changed my clothes but had wet my hair down and mussed it up considerably from the tightly sprayed "business look" into what I hoped was more like the tussled and thinning hair of a hard-working and slightly sad ranch hand. When I entered the holding area, I walked into the middle of a controversy. The casting director stepped out of her office and announced to the group that the batteries in their taping microphone had gone out during the audition of one of the actors who had gone in after me and they were checking the tapes to make sure when the sound problem had started.

When the casting director returned, she informed me that the battery problem had apparently started during the audition I had "nailed" and it would have to be re-shot. Unfortunately for me, I had already stuffed my dress shirt and suit pants into a wrinkled wad at the bottom of a closed backpack and my hair was now a stringy mess, I had basically gone through a full costume and makeup transformation.

Now, a lot of younger or less experienced actors might have panicked at this point. In fact, without mindfulness training, I might have freaked out myself (and I've been at this for 30 years). It was a high-pressure situation for a big TV show and I had to redo an already excellent audition after 12 hours on the road that included several hiccups and one downright meltdown. However, I went in the room, auditioned for the ranch hand (which went pretty well, too), marched straight to the bathroom, changed back into my jacket and tie (I stayed in the jeans since the shot would be framed above the waist), and went back in for round two of "well-dressed businessman." Did it go as well the second time? Not really, but with the full force of my concentration on the current moment in the audition room, it still went pretty well and was certainly an acceptable reading for the character.

I thanked the casting director and her staff, who by that time had been dealing with me for almost two hours, and caught an Uber back to the airport; just another day as a working actor.

There are several interesting lessons embedded in the above story. First, I was thoroughly familiar with each type of audition scenario I was asked to do that day. I had literally auditioned as a spokesperson, slightly comedic commercial character, and guest star on an hour-long TV drama hundreds of times in the past. So there was nothing about the actual audition situations that took me off guard nor surprised me in the least. As I have suggested, the basics of audition technique are prerequisites to becoming a professional actor and you should learn those elsewhere. What I teach in this book will help you do those things *better* under pressure.

The circumstances that affected me that day were several: forgetting lines (which happens to *everybody* sometimes), transportation issues, severely limited timeframes for preparation, and unexpected opportunities piling on top of each other without warning (basically scheduling issues). *None of these has to do with audition technique.* All of those circumstances were *beyond my control* and were indeed external stressors. The only way to deal with things beyond your control that may cause you stress or distraction in an audition session is to make yourself *distraction and stress proof* to begin with. And that is basically what the rest of this book is about.

4 SELF-CARE: LEARNING TO TUNE YOUR INSTRUMENT

If you are serious about being an actor at any level— student, amateur, or professional—self-care is one of the most important tools you have at your disposal. This is true because if both your body and your mind are not functioning harmoniously and at their peak potentials, you will never give your very best audition or performance. It's that simple.

What do I mean by "self-care"? Wikipedia defines it as "any necessary human regulatory function which is under individual control, deliberate and self-initiated." For the actor, this can include diet and exercise, ongoing physical and vocal training, grooming and appearance, and so forth. But I want to add a few things to that traditional list that you may not have considered before:

- Mental hygiene

- Attentional training

- Relaxation exercises

All of these are important because they help address the three main impediments to successful auditioning that we discussed in the last chapter. If you are not already doing these three forms of self-care in your daily life, then you are not functioning at the top of your game. If your mind is cluttered, you are an emotional wreck, or you are uptight and jittery, you will not be able to effectively deploy your attention in the present moment and give your very best audition.

Many schools of actor training look at the actor through "the instrumental model." In general, this model postulates that the actor's "instrument" (much like a musical instrument for a musician) is made up of body, voice, and cognition (also called imagination). Further, said instrument's components, body/voice/imagination, are trained through activities like movement work, vocal and speech techniques, and analytic and imaginative exercises, respectively. If your instrument is not properly "tuned," you will not be able to deliver a top-notch performance. This is where self-care comes in. Let's take each of these areas individually.

Mental Hygiene

Mental hygiene, in our context, means your basic psychological functioning. Are you psychologically stable? Do you have mood swings or difficulty controlling your emotions? Have you ever had trouble with depression or other mental conditions that have caused you problems? Do you have substance abuse issues? Any untreated condition that you might have that prevents you from being rigorously self-aware and honest with yourself could be holding you back from becoming the actor you want to be. Therefore, one practical action that an actor can take is to deal with any outstanding emotional or mental difficulties before subjecting themselves to the intensity and stress that almost always comes along with an acting career.

There are many counselors and psychologists today who help people through what is called *growth counseling* (sometimes called humanistic psychology or positive psychology).

Growth counseling can also be offered by career or success coaches. Growth counseling essentially uses techniques developed in the practice of psychotherapy and applies them to healthy individuals in order to facilitate psychological growth and the fulfilment of individual potential. An evaluation by, and perhaps even a few sessions with, a growth-oriented counselor or coach can be very useful for clearing up any minor psychological or social issues you might be experiencing that could limit you as an actor. I'm not suggesting heavy psychoanalysis or anything similar, just a minor tune-up that can help you clear away any non-helpful personal problems. That is one way to enact good "mental hygiene."

There are also a few very good books on what is known as "positive psychology." For actors interested in removing blocks to success and performing at their highest potential, I strongly recommend reading the following books:

Flow: The Psychology of Optimal Experience, Csikszentmihalyi, M. (1990).

Creativity: Flow and the Psychology of Discovery and Invention, Csikszentmihalyi, M. (1996).

Authentic Happiness: Using the New Positive Psychology to Realize Your Potential for Lasting Fulfillment, Seligman, M. E. P. (2002).

For a more complete list of psychology books that are basic to actor training and audition technique, please see the *Audition Basics Toolkit* available for free download on my website, www.KevinPage.com.

Attentional Training

Last year I interviewed Richard Feldman, current head of the acting program at the Julliard School in New York City, and he explained that "there has to be a level of conscious awareness about your instrument [as an actor] that a regular person doesn't have to have. ... Full *present-ness* and a point of *focus* in a field of awareness is of the highest, highest value [to the actor]" (2017).

It turns out that the ability to focus your attention in the field of your own awareness can be trained. This training, in the broadest of senses, is usually called *meditation practice* (or sometimes *mindfulness*) and has been used by yogis and spiritual seekers for more than 2,500 years. But it has only been in the last 50 years or so that modern Western science, through both psychology and neuroscience, has become interested in this phenomenon. Scientific research into the effects of meditation training has genuinely exploded in the last 20 years, and now there are studies into all kinds of areas that previously had been ignored or even ridiculed by scientists.

Recent research has demonstrated a positive effect from various forms of meditation practice on such diverse areas as depression, pain management, motivation, job performance, self-image and anxiety, even performance on college entrance exams. The press has picked up on this mania so that it seems like there is a new news report about additional findings every day. For a detailed look at much of this research and the application of meditative practice in an acting conservatory setting, see my upcoming book, *Advanced Consciousness Training for Actors: Meditation Techniques for the Performing Artist* (Routledge Press, September, 2018). In the book, I detail an entire program of meditation training for the serious acting student or professional. I will introduce many of the same techniques in this book in a form that can directly help you in the audition process.

The main point is that attentional training is no longer optional in today's competitive acting environment. And the bottom line is this: If you actually *do* the exercises in this book on a regular basis, you will *book more jobs* in the actual workplace.

Relaxation Exercises

Relaxation and an accompanying sense of self-confidence are absolute necessities for the auditioning actor. And, luckily, there are specific types of meditation practice (see Chapter Five) that can help you cultivate that perfect state of relaxation anywhere and anytime you choose (including the audition room). That ability alone should be worth the price you paid for this book!

Many actors struggle with tension in their bodies and negative "self-talk" or self-criticism before, during, and after an audition session. None of this is helpful and, I would argue that nervousness and negativity are most often the root causes of failed auditions. In addition to the meditation training I will offer in this book, I also have several exercises that are designed specifically to improve self-confidence and reduce nervousness *on command*. Once again, these exercises are based on very old principles, but it has been only recently that science has been able to verify their positive effects.

Much more than just telling yourself to relax, it is important for the actor to be able to predictably enter a state of relaxation even when a "normal person" would be on pins and needles; it is just what good actors do. This book can help you with that.

So, if you are looking at your "actor's instrument" (mind/body/voice), you can understand the self-care activities introduced in this book as the maintenance and tuning of that instrument for an optimal performance. After all, you would not expect a concert violinist to walk out onto a performance stage without having first both carefully tuned her instrument and practiced her piece of music until it flowed effortlessly. Why should it be any different for the auditioning actor? As Richard Feldman explained above, actors *must* have a level of conscious awareness about their instrument that regular people don't have—and that is why self-care is not optional.

5 EVERY AUDITION BEGINS WITH
A BREATH

Even though I have already explained that much of what I present in this book is based on traditional meditation and mindfulness practices, I am going to use slightly different language to talk about what we will be doing. From this point on, I will be introducing practical exercises that are either "attentional" or "intentional" in nature.

Attentional exercises, for our purposes, are intended to strengthen the attention function; in other words, your ability to deploy and focus attention where you want it. Intentional exercises are intended to adjust or alter your perceptions of what you do and who you are in a way that will make you more confident and less self-critical (which, in turn, will reduce any tendency to get nervous in the audition situation).

Let's start with a simple test to assess your current attentional abilities.

The Metronome Exercise

Instructions:

- Get a real metronome (a stopwatch with a second hand will work) and place it where you have a clear view of the moving arm/hand.

- Alternatively, you can download a metronome or stopwatch app onto your smart phone. If you do, make sure to use the graphic view (with the moving bar or second hand), NOT the digital numbers display.

- Find a quiet spot where you will not be disturbed or distracted for at least 5 minutes.

- Relax and clear your mind.

- Turn on the metronome or stop watch and follow the moving hand with your eyes for 5 minutes.

- Keep following the movement of the metronome or watch hand for the entire 5 minutes.

- Do not allow any other thoughts to enter your head. Just keep focused on the movement that you are following with your eyes.

- If you find that you have become distracted or are thinking about anything other than the movement of the device before you, you have failed the test and must start over.

- Stay with the movement of the metronome without losing focus for the full 5 minutes.

How did you do? Was it easy for you to stay with the exercise for the full 5 minutes or did you find your attention wandering? Did you become distracted by thoughts or external noises and have to start over? Or was it easy to maintain a concentrated focus of attention for five minutes without wavering?

Most people (and this includes actors) who have not engaged in some form of attentional training will not be able to successfully complete this exercise. It turns out that, without training, the human mind has difficulty focusing on one thing for even a short five-minute interval.

Now, ask yourself this question: How many scenes that you have been in, on stage or film, are less than five minutes? Even most auditions last longer than this if you count the time from when you arrive at the casting studio until the time you leave the building! So, is it a problem if you can't even pay attention to what you are doing (and a simple assignment at that, watching a clock hand) for five minutes? I argue that actors who have exceptional abilities to focus their attention are at a great *advantage* over those who cannot, regardless of the content of the play or audition sides.

Let's try another test, one that is much simpler, and see just how strong your current powers of attention are.

The Silent Chair Test

Instructions:

- You will need an egg timer or digital alarm for this exercise, preferably one that is silent and does not make a ticking or vibrating sound.

- Locate a comfortable chair or couch where you can sit undisturbed for at least 20 minutes.

- You can also lie down if that would be more comfortable, but do not close your eyes because that can lead to sleep.

- The room should be quiet. It is best to do this exercise alone or where everyone in the room is participating at the same time.

- Set the timer for 20 minutes.

- Sit (or lie down) with your back fairly straight and your arms resting by your sides or with your hands in your lap.

- Your eyes should remain open and gently focused on a spot perhaps 4 to 6 feet in front of you (or on the ceiling). This is a "soft focus" not a hard stare. You simply want to stay awake and alert throughout the exercise, without strain of any kind.

- Now, clear your mind of any thoughts or concerns, and just relax in the present moment. Think of nothing.

- Sit for 20 minutes without becoming distracted by thoughts or sounds. Do not look at the timer until it goes off, indicating the conclusion of the exercise.

- If you find that you have become distracted or that your thoughts have wandered, simply clear your mind, relax once again, and continue to sit in silence without moving, shifting your weight, or thinking about anything until the timer goes off.

Again, how did you do? Was it easy for you to sit in relaxed silence for 20 minutes or did your thoughts start racing around in circles?

As with the Metronome Exercise, most people that have not had previous attentional or meditation training find it difficult to complete this exercise. Some may even find it uncomfortable.

So, I ask you again: Wouldn't you expect an actor who could win an audition and subsequently play a leading role in a film or TV series to be able to pay attention to what they were doing for at least 20 minutes without becoming overwhelmingly distracted? I sure would. Most of the rest of this book will teach you how to gain a superior level of control over your attention and ability to focus that attention where you want it.

The Attention Function

There are two types of attention. One we will call "concentrated attention," which involves focusing all of your conscious awareness on a single object and holding it there through a force of will. This is the most common type of attentional exercise used by beginning meditators and will be a main focus of our work for the first several weeks. In the next exercise, for example, you will practice a particular type of concentration of attention exercise.

The other type of attention we call "open awareness," which involves being aware of all of your experience in the current moment without judging or grasping at any particular element of that experience. In other words, open awareness is attention focused on "the whole present moment" instead of a particular object within the present moment, as with concentrated attention. This concept can be a little more difficult to grasp and that is why, in part, we will start with concentration of attention exercises and work our way into open awareness exercises (sometimes called "mindfulness").

On the whole, what we will be doing in the following pages is training the attention function (made up of both kinds of attentional focus: concentrated and open awareness) so that it can be deployed intentionally and with greater control, which is at the heart of every great performance or audition.

This program of training will take some time. But like with any kind of training (weightlifting, for instance), the amount of benefit you experience is in direct proportion to the amount of genuine, disciplined effort you put into it. Weightlifting is actually a good analogy for the kind of attentional training we will be engaging in. If you think of your attention span like a set of untrained muscles, then just like for the bodybuilder, it will probably take several trips to the gym over several months before you will be able to show noticeably different shapes and contours of those muscle groups. You might feel great after your workouts in only a few sessions, and start to get physically stronger by the day, but to really put on inches of lean muscle mass takes sustained effort over time.

So let's think about our attention training like a bodybuilding program and the following exercise like the bench press, a basic exercise to build mass and strength. We can work on refining it later; but for now, let's add some bulk!

Attentional Exercise #1: Counting Your Breath

In the Silent Chair Test above, you sat comfortably in silence for 20 minutes and tried to "think of nothing." That didn't work very well, did it? Part of the reason why is that the mind loves to wander. It is like a little puppy dog exploring its environment, sniffing from this shoe, to that chew toy, to this ball of dust, and back to the shoe; always curious, always moving around. That is natural. That is just what minds do.

Our purpose with attentional training is not to stop thoughts (which only actually happens when you die), but to become less attached to them, to follow them less readily when they arise at random. This may sound like an impossible task after the previous two exercises, but I assure you, with practice, you will be able to alter your relationship to your own thoughts in a way that will allow you much better control over *where* your attention is drawn at any given moment. And *that* is the holy grail for the actor.

Note that this exercise is very similar to the Silent Chair Test you already did; however, instead of trying to think of nothing (which is basically impossible), you will be focusing your attention on the simplest of physical functions: Your breathing. The initial instructions are nearly identical to those for the Silent Chair, but please read through to the end and make sure you understand the important differences before you begin.

Instructions:

- You will need an egg timer or digital alarm for this exercise, preferably one that is silent and does not make a ticking or vibrating sound.

- Locate a comfortable chair or couch where you can sit undisturbed for at least 20 minutes.

- You can also lie down, if that would be more comfortable, but do not close your eyes because that can lead to sleep.

- The room should be quiet. It is best to do this exercise alone or where everyone in the room is participating at the same time.

- Set the timer for 20 minutes.

- Sit (or lie down) with your back fairly straight and your arms resting by your sides or with your hands in your lap.

- Your eyes should remain open and gently focused on a spot perhaps 4 to 6 feet in front of you (or on the ceiling). This is a "soft focus," not a hard stare. You simply want to stay awake and alert throughout the exercise, without strain of any kind.

- Settle into your position and allow your attention to turn inward. Take a few deep breaths and then breath normally.

- Breath in and out through your nose, keeping the mouth shut and allowing the tongue to rest comfortably against the back of your front teeth (this will keep you from over salivating and needing to swallow often).

- Become aware of the sensation of your breathing.

- Pay careful attention to the sensation of coolness as the air enters the nostrils, the gentle rising of your belly as you fill yourself with life-giving air, and the rising of your chest as the act of inhaling completes. Now follow the physical sensation of the exhale as the chest then the belly deflate and the breathing cycle completes.

- On the next inhale, while again following each sensation as it arises, silently count in your mind, "one." Then, as the chest once again begins to fall on the exhale, count "two," so that you are silently counting each inhale and exhale as it occurs.

- Continue to count each inhale and exhale as you experience the physical sensations of your breathing pattern until you reach the number ten (5 full breathing cycles), and then start again with "one" on your next inhale.

- If at any point during the session you lose track of the count or become distracted by external sensations or wandering thoughts, gently let those thoughts or sensations go, return your attention to the sensation of your breath, and begin your count again with the very next inhale.

- Continue to physically and mentally relax as you sit and silently count your inhales and exhales from one to ten.

- Once again, if your mind wanders or you become distracted, avoid any self-judgement or negative self-talk and simply return to the breath.

> • When the timer goes off, your session has ended and you may allow your attention to expand to take in the room around you.

So, how did this session go? Was it easier to stay focused on your breath than trying to have an empty mind? You will almost certainly have gotten distracted (more than once) and had to begin the count over from one. This is common and natural. In fact, one of the main points of this exercise is to *practice returning the attention to a single object* (in this case, the sensation of the breath in the body). So, in many ways, those moments of distraction are actually part of the exercise. Don't let the hyperactive puppy that is your mind frustrate you; its job is to wander around and explore its environment. We are simply training this puppy to return to its blanket every time it wanders off so that eventually it will know its most comfortable and safe spot in the house to rest.

Some people report that this kind of attentional exercise actually makes their thoughts race. Much more likely, however, the reason you are confronted with racing thoughts is that you have previously been unaware of them until you sat down and tried to focus your attention on something simple like your breathing! Becoming aware of you own thinking is a very important part of attentional training. After all, how effective as an actor do you suppose you will be if your mind is running all over the place like a puppy and you are not even aware of it?

If you discover racing thoughts when you do this breathing exercise, do not panic or worry. First, as I said above, this discovery is perfectly normal and even expected at the start. Second, as you continue to practice the Counting Breaths Exercise, your thoughts will eventually begin to calm and you will find that it is quite easy, even pleasant, to count your breaths in an unbroken string.

Counting Your Breaths is a basic attentional training exercise and should be repeated daily for 20-minute sessions.

Regularity is more important than quantity, particularly when you start. If you are finding it difficult to work a 20-minute session into your schedule, try getting up a few minutes earlier in the mornings and do it first thing (maybe while your coffee is brewing?). This exercise alone, if done on a regular basis for an extended period of time, can actually transform your ability to focus and direct your attention and improve your acting and auditioning skills noticeably.

In the next chapter, I will introduce some of the apps and digital devices that can make starting an attentional training practice easier.

6 INTERLUDE TWO: APPS AND GADGETS (TO GET YOU STARTED)

Over the past few years, there has been an explosion of new devices and apps for mobile phones that help people get started on a meditation or mindfulness (or attentional training) practice. On the whole, these are very useful ways for beginners to establish a practice that they otherwise might not engage in. However, over time, the serious actor will eventually leave these apps and gadgets behind for the simple silence of a breathing practice, as introduced in the last chapter. So keep in mind that, in the long run of your career, you will only use what follows as a starting block to launch your efforts (and you can skip this step altogether if you like).

Headspace and Calm are currently two of the most popular meditation apps for digital devices. I will look at both of them in detail below.

Headspace

Headspace is a digital service that provides guided meditation sessions and mindfulness training. Its content can be accessed online or via their mobile apps. In April 2016, Headspace claimed to have over 6 million people using their programs.

Headspace was founded in 2010 by Andy Puddicombe, a former Buddhist monk, and Rich Pierson, a marketing and brand development executive. To date, the company has raised over $30 million dollars and its training app is considered one of the most successful apps in the mindfulness space.

The Headspace app takes a "gamification" approach to getting people involved with meditation practice. You can try it for free (for up to 10 days), but then the program requires a paid subscription to continue on. In my book, *Advanced Consciousness Training (A.C.T.) for Actors: Meditation Techniques for the Performing Artist* (Routledge, 2018), I recommend that conservatory actors (those who are in serious daily actor training for 2-3 years) only use this type of program as a *starting point* and to transition to the non-guided, silent versions of self-directed practice as soon as they can. The reason for this is, while Headspace is a great way to establish a regular daily attentional training practice, it also requires a computer or digital device, and the constant videos and audio narration are actually distracting once you've learned the techniques. Also, the platform becomes more about *interacting with the platform* than spending significant periods in quiet, focused training (something absolutely necessary for the successful actor in today's competitive climate). So, with those caveats in mind, I will walk you through a brief introduction to the Headspace app and let you be your own judge as to its usefulness in your situation.

When you first sign up for the Headspace app, you are immediately greeted by a simple video that gives the basic instructions for a seated meditation, similar to the ones I presented at the end of the last chapter. Most of Headspace's videos are animated in a light and amusing style that makes these beginning phases easy to understand as well as entertaining.

Once the video is complete, you are offered a guided

version of a three-minute mindfulness meditation. This very short session is narrated by Puddicombe himself and mostly focuses on an awareness of the breath and the physical sensations of breathing. Once complete you are offered a chance to see your results on a type of dashboard page that promises to track your progress over the next nine days as you work your way through the "basics" unit of the Headspace app by logging on once a day to practice another guided meditation. The sessions, of course, become longer and move in a simple, understandable progression.

Once you have completed the 10-day basics program, you are invited to subscribe to Headspace by opening a full account attached to your credit card. It costs around $8.00 a month (if you commit to a year of the service up front); $12.99 per month if you pay monthly (but you will have to remember to cancel your subscription if you decide you don't need the guided versions of the meditation any more); or you can pay nearly $400 for a "lifetime" subscription. Again, you will need to decide whether a guided, structured program (sort of like a "meditation diet" in a way) is worth the money, particularly when versions of very similar guided meditation sessions are available from thousands of sources on the internet for free (including my website, www.KevinPage.com, under the Meditation Tools tab).

Once you subscribe to Headspace, you can choose how you want to structure you own program. The app offers "packs," which are progressions of guided sessions similar to the introductory 10-day basics pack you complete first, and "singles," which are meditation sessions intended to cultivate different states of mind or assist with activities, such as falling asleep, commuting, or dealing with moments of anxiety and stress.

According to Wikipedia, Headspace content is clustered into four areas once users have completed the Foundation stage—health, performance, relationships and Headspace

Pro. Users are asked to complete and master a level of meditation before they can move on to the more advanced section. Each session is about ten minutes long, usually in a video format.

The app is set up so that users complete one session (one meditation) every day for ten days. After ten days, a series is completed. Currently packs include Foundation, Sports, Health, Relationships, Performance, and Headspace Pro. Each pack series after the introductory series has different categories and meditation tasks for you to complete. Users are not able to preview other categories' sessions until they have "unlocked them" by completing the sessions up to that point (making the app a bit like a video game). Additionally, the app features a subsection of meditation specifically for kids. These are short meditations range from one to five minutes and are applicable for children from toddlers to preteens.

The core of the Headspace approach is to use guided meditation exercises to accomplish a number of different general goals. These are narrated meditation sessions in which a "leader" talks the meditator through the session. This is an excellent way to learn the basic instructions, but for more advanced students (like you will be by the time you finish this book), the narration can be a distraction. The greatest value of a program like Headspace is in helping you develop a regular habit of practice. However, as almost all of their guided meditations run for only 10 minutes or less, it is difficult to build any true momentum or to significantly strengthen your attention function.

The focus of the program for actors that I present in *Advanced Consciousness Training (A.C.T.) for Actors,* as well as in this book, is on self-guided, internalized meditation practices intended specifically to improve concentration skills, reduce nervousness in the audition session, and increase access to "the present moment" of performance. These are very specific goal sets. All three of these specialized areas are better served, in the long run, by internally focused attention work, that you will learn in the following chapters, more than on a platform that tries to offer "something for everyone" in a simplified package.

If you want to use a program like Headspace to get started, great! However, I would encourage you to eventually migrate back to the self-directed work, whether it is from this book or some other source, that focuses primarily on rigorous attentional training rather than a broad menu of general activities. For your purposes, deep and narrow practice will be preferable to broad and comprehensive libraries of experiences.

Calm

Calm is another highly popular meditation instruction app. It is both similar to and different from Headspace. Calm uses a female narrator with a cheery, enthusiastic voice. The "basics" Calm series, very much like that of Headspace, is a 7-day progression, starting with a 3-minute session and working up to a 12-minute session on Day Seven. At this point, you are encouraged to join the subscription model by, once again, inputting your credit card for monthly or annual charging cycles. Calm is about a dollar more a month than Headspace if you choose month-to-month billing, but cheaper if you sign up for annual billing or a single life-time charge of $299.

Calm focuses more on offering multiple styles of meditation from which you can build your own program. Some of their cool features include "Sleep Stories," which are bedtime stories for adults read by professional readers with dulcet and relaxing voices. And, on the main page of the mobile app, you will find the "Breathe Circle," which encourages you to time your breathing cycle to a slow and steady pace by following a graphic timer. However, the basic Calm program is still built on guided meditations intended for short and informal use and, as such, the app has the same limitations as Headspace when it comes to using it as a tool for more serious attentional training specifically for actors.

As with Headspace, if you need something to motivate you getting started with a meditation practice, I say choose the app you find most pleasant; but once you are in the daily habit, plan to take the work more seriously and come back here for further instruction. As I have mentioned in other places, guided versions of the types of attentional training I have developed specifically for actors are available on my website (for free) at www.KevinPage.com (under the Meditation Tools tab).

Muse

Muse is a $299 biofeedback device that measures brain wave activity through a fitted plastic headband embedded with seven electroencephalography (EEG) sensors that monitor your brain and transmit that data, using Bluetooth radio waves, to an app on your smart phone. The app then gives you feedback using soundscapes and imagery on your phone to help you target and identify "states of relaxation." The theory is that, wearing the device while meditating, can help "guide" you toward deeper, more relaxing meditative states.

In practice, the Muse head set is simple to use and the app has an orientation session that helps you calibrate the device to your body each time it runs. Muse offers a series of guided meditations, some of which are led by well-known personalities like Deepak Chopra, and a series of "soundscapes" that adapt to the data your brainwaves provide.

For example, Muse has an ocean soundscape that starts with the sounds of waves crashing on a beach. Depending on how agitated your brainwaves are, the waves will be relatively loud and crashing like the sound of an approaching storm. But as you sit in silence, ostensibly trying to meditate to calm your brainwaves, the sounds of the waves on the shore become more calm and sedate. When you reach a certain level of brainwave sedation, birds begin to tweet along the shore, indicating that you have "attained a meditative state." The more birds you can get to chirp by deepening your calm, the better.

Like the other apps we have discussed, there is a subscription "premium" version of the app that unlocks additional guided meditations, soundscapes, and tracking functions so that you can build a progressive program of meditation training based on your own needs. And, like the other apps described, this can be a fun and entertaining way to start a regular meditation practice. However, once again, for those that take the work seriously and extend their practice over time, the sound games and guided meditations ultimately become a distraction to the deeper purpose of building superior powers of concentration that we are looking for as actors.

If you have the money to spare, Muse is a highly entertaining introduction to meditative practice that, while perhaps not necessary, is genuinely fun!

In the next chapter, I will introduce some additional exercises that can extend your attentional training beyond the "silent chair" and out into your daily activities, thus expanding your opportunities to work on your attention function.

7 ATTENTION WITHIN THE BODY

Having tested your own attention spans, learned a traditional attentional training technique (counting breathes), and reviewed several devices and apps that can help establish a daily practice habit, it is now time to look at some additional exercises that, when combined with counting breaths, can be used as a basic long-term program for improving your "instrument" as an actor.

Hopefully, by this time you have been able to use a combination of apps or simple seated breath-counting to establish a habit of spending 20 minutes (or more) per day training your attention function. Now, I am going to share additional traditional concentration exercises that can be added to or rotated with the counting of breaths to give you a menu to choose from in your personal training.

Some people find sitting very still in silence, even for only 20 minutes, difficult to do. In fact, it is difficult for almost everyone at first. However, with daily practice, it gets much easier. Even so, it can still be useful to learn other methods of training the puppy dog of your attentional function to calm down and stay where you want it. Remember what Richard Feldman (from Julliard) and many other master acting teachers say: *The ability to focus attention is critical for the successful actor!* So please do stick with the counting breaths exercise on a regular basis, even as we learn these new forms of concentration practice. I recommend (and practice myself) at least 20 minutes a day of silent, seated meditation regardless of whether I am using these additional forms. Seated meditation practice (counting breaths) is the core of this work; so even if it is difficult, stick with it!

The Traditional "Body Scan"

One of the most popular forms of meditation practice in the U.S. is called MBSR (which stands for Mindfulness-Based Stress Reduction). MBSR is a medicalized version of mindfulness training that takes the original exercises out of their Buddhist context (much as I have done in this book) and adapts them for use by adult medical patients, many of whom suffer from serious diseases and chronic pain.

One of the first exercises presented in the MBSR program is called the "Body Scan." In the body scan exercise, people usually lie on the floor, with a couple of pillows to support the head and knees, and close their eyes. Although the exercise can also be done sitting up and with eyes open (as I will suggest below), most people try this lying down to take full advantage of the relaxation benefits.

My version of this exercise is called "Attention Within the Body," or sometimes "Consciousness of the Body," and varies only in its focus on the attention function over pure relaxation and pain reduction. Nonetheless, most actors who first try this exercise fall asleep, which is perfectly natural.

For the Attention Within the Body exercise, you will be taking the entire body, mostly in its component parts, as your object of attention instead of the physical sensation of breathing. This exercise will take approximately 30 minutes to complete and should be done in a quiet, well-ventilated space where you (or the group) can be undisturbed for the entire duration of the exercise. Distractions or pauses during the exercise are strongly discouraged, as stopping and restarting is precisely the sort of distraction from concentration we are trying to remedy.

Instructions:

No cellphones or digital devices should be present in the room during this exercise because even vibration alerts are distracting. So, power the devices completely off and put them away, out of sight, before the session begins.

Sit on the floor on a cushion or mat and a meditation pillow to elevate your buttocks slightly above your knees (if you are sitting cross-legged). You can also sit on a chair with your feet on the ground in front of you, a shoulder-width apart. Place your hands palms up in your lap, right hand cradling left, with thumb tips lightly touching. Your hands and arms should be relaxed. You can also place your hands palms down on your knees. Once you've found your position, settle in and allow your awareness to turn inward.

You can also lie on the floor for this exercise. You may want to use a yoga mat and some low pillows to support your neck and slightly raise the knees. Place your hands comfortably at your sides, palms either up or down. Hands can also be draped lightly on top of your abdomen, but avoid interlocking the fingers. The goal, whether seated or lying down, is to remain comfortably in this position for half an hour or more without the need to overly shift or adjust your position. Relaxation will be an integral part of this exercise.

While you can close your eyes, I recommend keeping them open and softly focused. If you are seated, you can let your eyelids droop slightly and pick a spot on the floor between 3 and 5 feet in front of you, where you can focus without straining. Again, you want a soft focus so that you are able to see the objects in your immediate field of vision even though individual objects may be slightly blurred. If you are lying down, pick an area of the ceiling (or sky) that you can gaze upon easily without staring. The point is to stay awake and alert for the duration of the exercise without falling asleep or causing tension in the eyes. If you choose to close your eyes, be warned that this can lead to sleep, which is not our goal (although it often happens, particularly at first); and so, if you find yourself drifting out of consciousness, you may want to open your eyes, blink a few times, and maintain a soft focus as you continue.

Unless you otherwise cannot, due to blocked airways or the like, it is recommended that you keep your mouth closed during all attention training exercises and breathe through your nose. While your mouth is closed, allow your tongue to rest, pressed gently against your front teeth. This will prevent excessive salivation and swallowing, which can be a distraction during extended sessions.

Awareness Within the Body is a "guided" meditation practice, meaning that a narrator or leader will direct your focus during the course of the exercise. This direction can be read from the following script by someone who has volunteered to lead the group, or you can listen to recorded versions that are available for free on the internet from multiple sources, including my website, www.KevinPage.com. If you are working alone, you can also record a version of the following script and then play it back while following the instructions. Note, if you make your own recording, be sure to leave enough time in the pauses to allow yourself to fully experience the given activity; do not rush.

Attention Within the Body Guidance Script:

- Take a moment to settle into your body. Release any tension and allow your awareness to focus on your breathing.

- Simply experience your body breathing for the next few breaths. (Pause.)

- Now imagine that your attention is a bright spotlight bathing your entire body in warm light. Let the light wash away any tensions that remain until you are entirely relaxed, just breathing in this moment.

- And now let the spotlight of your attention focus into a tight beam and travel down the left side of your body to focus just on your left foot.

- Continue to breathe, but allow your attention to stay focused on the left foot.

- What does your left foot feel like? Flex your toes and rotate your ankle gently. Let all of your awareness be with your left foot for a few breaths. (Pause.)

- Now the spotlight of your awareness becomes a tight beam focused only on your left big toe. Bring all of your attention onto your left big toe and just experience any sensations you might find there. (Pause.)

- And now the beam of your attention widens to take in all of the toes on your left foot. Sense each toe in order. Can you feel the skin in between your toes? What is the difference between the top and bottom of your toes? Are your toes warm or cold? Just let your awareness explore the toes of your left foot for a while as you continue to breathe and relax. (Pause.)

- Now let your spotlight of attention flow down to the ball of your foot. What does that feel like? Breathe into the ball of your left foot and release any tension you find there. (Pause.)

- Now move the attention to the blade and the arch of the left foot. How does that feel? Can you sense the difference from one side of your foot to the other? Breathe into the center of your foot.

- Now allow your attention to focus on the heel of your foot. Breathe into the heel of your foot. See if you can sense the back of your ankle, where the Achilles tendon connects to your heel. (Pause.)

- Widen your awareness now to take in the entire foot. Breathe into your left foot and experience what that is like for a moment. (Pause.)

- With the next breath, let the spotlight of your attention flow up to your calf. Breathe into your left calf. Just experience your calf for a moment. Feel the back of your calf. And now move your attention to the front of your shin. Just breathe and be with your lower leg for a moment.

- Now let your spotlight move up to your left knee. Breathe into your left knee. Sense the knee cap. Sense the back of your knee.

- Allow the spotlight of your awareness to move up to your left thigh. Feel the top of your thigh from the kneecap up to your hip. Let your attention flow around to the bottom of your thigh, moving along your hamstring and up to your buttock.

- Now let your attention move into your pelvis. Breathe into your pelvis. Feel your connection with the chair or floor. Relax your pelvic area and just breathe for a moment.

- And with the next breath, let the spotlight of your attention flow down your right leg and focus on your right foot. As you did with your left foot, let your attention focus into a tight beam all the way down on your right big toe. Breath into your right big toe. Feel the difference between your big toe and your other toes; the skin between them. Wiggle them one time and then simply breathe.

- And now let your attention move to the ball of your right foot. Breathe into the ball of your right foot. (Pause.)

- Move your attention to the blade and the arch of the right foot. Sense the difference from one side of your foot to the other. Breathe into the center of your foot and let any tension you find there dissolve.

- Now allow your attention to flow into the heel of your right foot. Breathe into the heel of your foot. Sense the back of your ankle, the Achilles tendon.

- Move your attention to the top of your right foot. Now around to the bottom and widening your spotlight of awareness, take in the entire right foot, all bathed in a soft, glowing light. (Pause.)

- With the next breath, let your attention move up to your right calf. Fully experience your calf for a moment. Feel the back of your calf. And now move your attention to the front of your shin. Just breathe and be with your lower leg for a moment.

- Move your attention up to your right knee. Sense the knee cap. Sense the back of your knee.

- Allow your awareness to move up to your thigh. Feel the top of your right thigh. Let your attention flow around to the bottom of your thigh, moving along your hamstring and up to your buttock with each new breath. (Pause.)

- Now let your attention move once more into your pelvis. Breathe into your pelvis. And for just a moment, let your awareness fill the entire lower part of your body, letting go of any tensions you might find there. (Pause.)

- With the next breath, let the spotlight of your awareness move up to your left hand and focus there. Feel it cradled in your right hand or gently resting on your knee. Now focus your beam onto your left thumb. Let all of your attention focus in the tip of your left thumb for a moment. See if you can feel the thumbnail. (Pause.) Now move your beam to the fore finger ... the middle finger ... the ring finger ... and finally, the little finger. See if you can hold your attention just on the fingers and thumb of the left hand for a moment. (Pause.)

- Now let your awareness flow into the palm of your left hand. What sensations do you find there? Feel the back of your left hand, the contact with the skin of your right, or the sensation of air flowing over it. Let your left hand become very light and relaxed.

- Let your beam of awareness flow up onto your left forearm, moving slowly from your wrist to the elbow. Sense your elbow and the tender flesh at the crook of your arm.

- Allow your awareness to move onto your left bicep. Feel the warmth of your spotlight there. Now sense the back of your upper arm from the elbow to the shoulder. Breathe. (Pause.)

- Now bathe your left shoulder in the warm glow of your attention with every new inhalation.

- Your attention now flows down your right arm until it settles in your right hand. As you breathe, let your awareness focus into a tight beam on your right thumb. See if you can sense just the tip of your right thumb for a moment. (Pause.) Now move your attention to the fore finger ... the middle finger ... the ring finger ... and finally, the little finger. See if you can hold your attention just on the fingers and thumb of the right hand for a moment. (Pause.)

- Now let your awareness flow onto the palm of your right hand. Feel the slight weight of your left hand as it rests in your right palm, feel the contact with the skin. Let your right hand become warm with the glow of your spotlight.

- And let your awareness flow up onto your right forearm, moving slowly from your wrist to the elbow. Sense your elbow and the flesh at the crook of your right arm.

- Move your focus of attention onto your right bicep, just experiencing what's there, releasing any tension. Now sense the back of your upper arm from the elbow to the shoulder. Breathe. (Pause.)

- Bathe your right shoulder in the warm glow of your attention with every new inhalation. (Pause.)

- Now let the spotlight of your attention shine onto your head. Your head is like a balloon, inflating a little more with each intake of breath. Floating on your shoulders, nearly weightless. (Pause.)

- Imagine that there is a string attached to the very top of your head and that a balloon is floating at the end of the string, lightly pulling at the top of your head, lengthening your spine, raising the energy of your body towards the ceiling. (Pause). And just let your head float there for a moment. Breathing. Fully relaxed. Light as air. (Pause.)

- And now, let your spotlight of attention widen to take in your whole body once again. Bathing your arms … and hands … and legs … and feet … and torso in a warm, glowing light. Let your breathing fill your entire body for just a moment. Everything light. Everything relaxed.

- And when you are ready, let your attention release from your body to include the room around you, the sounds of your surroundings, and the presence of your friends. Open your eyes if they have been closed.

> Blink and look around. Feel free to stretch and move a bit as you come back to the here and now of *this* room in *this* moment.

When done at the proper pace and with sufficient pauses for the participants to indulge in the experience, this exercise should take between 30 and 45 minutes to complete. It is very common to become so relaxed that you fall asleep. This is normal. If you fall asleep, simply try keeping your eyes open next time, or sitting if you were lying down. Like with all meditative training, this exercise takes practice. Eventually, you will easily be able to follow the entire sequence and maintain your focus on the various body parts with easy-but-focused attention.

Eventually, you can do the Attention Within the Body exercise without the guidance narration and simply direct your attention throughout the body. As with most of the exercises I introduce in this book, the eventual goal is to do each of them wholly internally without any outside guidance or input whatsoever. However, that will come with practice.

8 MOVEMENT AND AWARENESS

So far we have focused on attentional training exercises that involve remaining very still and turning the whole of your attention inward toward some bodily sensation, such as the movement of breath or the feel of individual body parts at rest. These seated (or lying down) exercises are the core of an attentional training routine for actors to improve attentional control, reduce nervousness, and improve "in the moment" awareness during performances and auditions. Therefore, these types of concentrated attention exercises should *always be included* in your mind/body-training program. What comes next is meant to be *additive* to, not a replacement for, the first two exercises.

If you have been doing the concentration exercises introduced so far for a few weeks (or more), you have probably started to get better at catching your mind when it wanders and gently (without judgment) returning it to the point of focus. If you are still struggling, don't worry. Just keep practicing on a daily basis. Everyone's progress is different and even if it takes a while, I promise it will be worth it in the end. If your progress feels slow, make sure you are doing at least 20-minute sessions *every day*; don't skip if you can help it. You can even add a second 20-minute session later in your day (perhaps before bed) to reinforce the practice. Also, try to do your daily sessions around the same time each day if you can. In the early phases, consistency is more important than quantity.

Attention-based Movement

Now you will extend your intentional focus of attention to the activity of walking. In this simple movement exercise, the focus of attention goes from a single object, such as the breath or a particular body part, one at a time, to the collection of sensations involved in moving through space. Instead of directing your attention to one thing, you will direct it at a process that unfolds in time.

Walking meditation has some distinct advantages over seated or lying-down exercises. First of all, since you will be standing up and moving, even if slowly, you are much less likely to fall asleep while doing the work. Also, as you get better at doing these exercises and extend the timeframe of your practice, seated meditation can become physically uncomfortable after a while. (Try sitting without moving sometime for two hours straight and you will see what I mean!) Walking meditation can be added to an extended practice session to offer a break for the body while still concentrating the attention in a useful manner.

As usual for our attention training sessions, no active cellphones or digital devices should be present in the room, even vibration alerts are distracting. So, power the devices completely off and put them away, out of sight, before the session begins.

This exercise can be done in bare or stocking feet, avoid shoes if possible. A direct connection between the feet and the surface of the ground can be useful, but is not absolutely necessary.

Locate a space where you can walk at least 5 to 10 paces back and forth without having to avoid or interact with obstacles (including other meditators if working in a group). The exercise can be done inside or outside, but it is often best at the beginning to practice in a quiet and secure inside location where distractions and interruptions can be minimized.

This exercise is typically done at a fairly slow pace compared to normal daily walking. Slowing the process down, particularly at first, will make it easier to discern the sometimes-subtle movements and shifts in balance that occur during this activity. However, you can proceed at a pace that is comfortable for you as long as you are able to sense the movements that are the object of this exercise. Slowness is by no means a requirement.

Instructions:

- Take a standing position with feet a shoulder-width apart and settle into your chosen spot. Close your eyes for a moment.

- Become aware of your body in space. Notice how your body is balanced on this spot. Feel your feet in contact with the floor. Stand in alignment, feet relaxed but firmly planted, knees unlocked and slightly bent, pelvis tucked slightly under your torso, spine erect and arms loose at your sides, elbows slightly bent, hands relaxed and fingers slightly curled. Gently roll your shoulders a couple of times, allowing the chest to open as you settle into a relaxed, aligned position.

- Let your attention move to your breath. Feel the sensation of coolness at the tips of your nostrils as the air enters your body and travels through your lungs. Just follow the breath as you stand for a moment.

- Now open your eyes. Gaze with a soft focus at the floor a few feet in front of you.

- Let your attention gather in your feet. And when you are ready, take your first step forward with your right foot, remaining fully present to the experience of raising the foot, swinging it forward through space, and placing it again on the floor.

- Sense the shift in your weight onto the right foot. As your weight shifts, your back foot will roll forward until just the big toe is touching the ground.

- Now raise your left foot from the ground, swinging it forward through space, and then shift your weight onto that foot as your back (right) foot now rolls forward until just the big toe is touching the ground.

- Continue walking at your own slowly-measured pace for a few steps, keeping the attention fully in your feet as you move across the floor.

- When you come to the end of your path, carefully pivot, noting where the weight shifts and how your feet feel on the floor as you make your turn. staying conscious of every movement. And then walk back to your starting position, attentive to each individual step and its unique qualities.

- Continue your walk for the allotted time, staying mindful of each step, trying to discern the sensations and changes of balance as they occur. Remember that each step is unique. Savor each step. Try to experience it deeply.

- If at any time you find your thoughts have drifted from the sensations of your current step, simply acknowledge the thought or feeling or memory that has captured your attention, and gently but firmly bring your attention back to the very next step you take. Sense your contact with the floor. The shift in balance. The rolling through of the back foot until only the big toe is touching the ground.

- When the exercise time is up and you have returned to your starting place, once again center yourself on both feet, a shoulder-width apart, and come to rest. Close your eyes for a moment.

- Become aware of your body in space. Feel your feet in contact with the floor. Stand in alignment, feet relaxed but firmly planted, knees unlocked and slightly bent, pelvis tucked slightly under your torso, spine erect and arms loose at your sides, elbows slightly bent, hands relaxed and fingers slightly curled. Gently roll your shoulders a couple of times, allowing the chest to open as you settle into a relaxed, aligned position.

- Allow your attention to turn once more toward your breath, and just breathe for a few moments, savoring each unique breath, centered in this moment.

- When you are ready, slowly and gently, allow your awareness to expand to include the room around you, the activity in the space, and the presence of your friends.

The above instructions can be read allowed by a leader, if you are working in a group; recorded as a guidance script (prerecorded versions are available on the website www.KevinPage.com); or merely act as a guide for your internalized work. Once the basic instructions have been learned, it is easy to simply focus your attention on the activity of walking.

9 USING A MANTRA FOR LASER-FOCUS

Below, I will introduce you to a different kind of concentration of attention practice that uses a word or phrase (called "mantra") as its object instead of a single sensation or process of movement.

The basic idea of mantra practice is to pick a word or simple phrase and repeat it over and over again, focusing your attention on that word or phrase as the exclusive subject of awareness during the practice session. In mantra practice, the mantra can be repeated either silently or vocalized as a type of chant.

Mantra work can also be done at times throughout the day that are not part of a formal meditation session. This is called "informal practice" and is an excellent technique for extending your attentional training beyond the meditation bench or cushion.

Mantra practice was made popular in America during the 1960s through the introduction of Transcendental Meditation (TM), a type of mantra meditation practice. That movement's founder, Maharishi Mahesh Yogi, was an Indian mystic who toured the U.S. and Europe extensively, promoting TM practice as a path to self-improvement. Maharishi was the personal teacher of the Beatles and other international celebrities, which helped popularize the TM movement.

For our purposes, I have created a unique mantra practice for actors to use in training their attention for the audition process. I will show you in a later chapter how to use a mantra in preparation for a specific audition, but for now we will learn the basic concentration meditation version.

For basic mantra practice, one picks a word or phrase as the object of concentrated attention. For our version, we will use a nonsense phrase that has no innate meaning but is easy to memorize and repeat as a series of phonetic sounds. Our mantra will be "Om—nani—lali—rum (where "om" is one syllable, "lali" and "nani" are both two syllables, and "rum" is one syllable).

Om—nani—lali—rum, can be uttered on an 8-count, and then repeated over and over again silently, like humming a tune or repeating a poem. The point of using this nonsense phrase is to focus the attention on the act of repetition (which becomes the object), rather than on any particular meaning that you might associate with the words.

Mantra-based meditation tends to strengthen over time as the phrase becomes more familiar and more habituated. Do not confuse the term "habituated" with mind*less*ness. The focus of mantra work is always being aware in the present moment, as it is with all of the forms of practice we have already discussed; however, as the repetition of the mantra becomes ever more familiar, it can lead to surprisingly deep states of concentration of attention and presence in the moment (the main goal of our training here). In practice, the more familiar the mantra becomes, the more easily and quickly the attendant state of concentration can be conjured through its repetition, making the mantra an extremely accessible tool for attentional training.

Mantra meditation can take many forms, including seated, standing, or lying down, as well as walking and even jogging! It can be done silently or spoken aloud as a repetitive chant. Below, I give brief instructions for using a mantra for a seated concentration of attention exercise that can then be adapted to other physical postures or activities. The instructions are nearly identical to those for the other exercises we have learned so far, but I will repeat them again for your convenience.

Mantra meditation, once established, is usually not performed as a guided meditation; so once you understand the instructions, you may continue by yourself, usually for sessions lasting between 15 and 30 minutes.

Instructions:

No cellphones or digital devices should be present in the room during this exercise, even vibration alerts are distracting. So, power the devices completely off and put them away, out of sight, before the session begins.

Sit on the floor on a cushion or mat and a meditation pillow to elevate your buttocks slightly above your knees (if you are sitting cross-legged). You can also sit on a chair with your feet on the ground in front of you, a shoulder-width apart. Place your hands, palms up in your lap, right hand cradling left, with thumb tips lightly touching. Your hands and arms should be relaxed. You can also place your hands palms down on your knees. Once you've found your position, settle in and allow your awareness to turn inward.

While you can close your eyes, I recommend keeping them open and softly focused. If you are seated, you can let your eyelids droop slightly and pick a spot on the floor, between 3 and 5 feet in front of you, where you can focus without straining. Again, you want to have a soft focus so that you are able to see the objects in your immediate field of vision even though individual objects may be slightly blurred.

Unless you otherwise cannot, due to blocked airways or the like, it is recommended that you keep your mouth closed during all meditation exercises and breath through your nose. While your mouth is closed, allow your tongue to rest, pressed gently against your front teeth. This will prevent excessive salivation and swallowing, which can be a distraction during extended sessions.

Relax into position and turn your attention inward. You may want to take a few conscious breaths to center yourself.

- When you are ready, begin to repeat the mantra "Om—nani—lali—rum" silently to yourself.

- Choose a slow to moderate rhythm that seems neither rushed nor sluggish. The tones of the mantra are best left fairly monotone, although you can choose to have the last syllable lilt up. (There is an audio example on the website for this book, www.KevinPage.com.) The repetition should be in a continuous, deliberate "loop" with no discernable break between phrases.

- If it is helpful, you can begin the session by chanting the phrase out loud a few times to establish it in your head before fully internalizing it for your session. Speak each syllable distinctly and completely but without long pauses between syllables, so that the phrase flows smoothly and rhythmically in an effortless drone.

- As you repeat the mantra over and over, silently to yourself, make sure to remain present and attentive to each syllable as it repeats. The purpose of the exercise is identical to the breathing, body scan, and walking exercises, in that your attention to the object, in this case your mantra, is to remain steady and focused.

- When your mind wanders, gently and without judgment, bring it back to the next syllable of the mantra, or start again from the beginning if you have lost your place.

- Use a timer or session leader to track the time of the session so that you do not need to be concerned with checking the time or deciding when the session is over. If you pre-select the session length, this will eliminate the need to check the time, which would be an unnecessary distraction.

- When the timer or the session leader indicates the session is over, gently let the mantra fade from your mind. You may want to take a few measured, conscious breaths as your attention broadens to include your surroundings and activities in the room.

Many actors exercise their bodies regularly, often by jogging, walking, or using various aerobic fitness devices, such as climbing machines or treadmills. During these activities, it is not uncommon for exercisers to wear headphones and listen to music or other kinds of audio or even visual content as a *distraction* while working out. Mantra-exercise is intended to directly contradict this chronic, distracted behavior by returning a level of consciousness and concentration to the exercise process. If you do not currently exercise, mantra-exercise can be added to your daily routine as a healthy fitness and meditative alternative.

It is important to note that mantra-exercise is not intended to replace the other concentration practices we have already discussed. Seated, or lying down, concentration practices (such as Counting Your Breaths, Attention Within the Body, and Walking Meditation) are the core of attentional training and *should not* be exchanged or replaced by "informal practice." (Informal practice is anything that extends mindful awareness into your daily activities, such as exercise, eating, or even doing the dishes, all of which are legitimate forms of mindfulness practice but are not legitimate forms of concentration meditation.) For successful attentional training, an actor should always do at least 20 minutes a day of core concentration exercise and then *add* things like mantra-exercise to extend the amount of practice in any given day.

The first instruction for mantra-exercise (or any other kind of conscious fitness routine) is to eliminate all forms of digital entertainment and distraction during the exercise session and concentrate fully and intently on the activity at hand (this will also improve the quality and effectiveness of your workouts, giving you maximum benefit). Even if you are doing weightlifting or some other kind of intensive workout that is not conducive to adding a meditative element, the time that you spend consciously focused on your activity, and not on media multitasking, is a period out of your day that discourages instead of encourages distraction and is, thus, of some value simply for that reason.

Below, I will give the instructions for a basic mantra-exercise practice based on walking in an outside environment. The instructions can be adapted to all manner of sustained, repetitive aerobic exercise activities.

It is very difficult to conjure the appropriate amount of concentrative attention in group exercise activities except perhaps a group walk or run, where participants are all utilizing the practice simultaneously.

The practitioner should always be cognizant of any potential safety concerns and *discontinue any concentrated meditative focus if it will in any way compromise the safety of an activity.* This advice is particularly important if you choose to utilize exercise equipment or are in an environment that requires diligent attention to your surroundings, such as busy city streets or a weightlifting gym.

If you use an app or other device to track or monitor your exercise session, set it up before the session begins. With the exception of necessary heart rate monitoring, plan on not interacting with any data until after the workout is complete.

Do not use headphones or any other kind of auditory content input. Mantra-exercise is an attentional training exercise and, with the exception of the above-mentioned non-invasive data capture programs, all device interaction should be eliminated during the activity. Use this session as conscious device-free time during your day. Unless absolutely necessary, do not answer phones or texts during the session. If at all possible, it is recommended to leave all devices off, without the vibrate feature enabled, as any kind of device input during a meditation session, active or passive, is an unnecessary distraction.

If you are walking or jogging outside, I recommend using a closed walking path where available. Your route should be familiar and safe, without undue hazards, such as heavily trafficked intersections. A well-defined walking path through a natural environment is ideal.

If you are doing mantra-exercise with others, it is best to agree in advance to forgo all conversation until the activity is over.

Do whatever necessary warm-up activities you need. You may take a couple of silent moments to center yourself, turn your attention inward, and become aware of your breath.

Instructions:

- Begin your walking or jogging as you normally would. The pace of your exercise should be normal, not slowed or adapted as in walking meditation from the earlier chapter. For this version of mantra-exercise, use the "Om—nani—lali—rum" mantra. The focus of attention will primarily be on the *repetition of the mantra* and not on the physical sensations of the activity (such as in walking meditation).

- Begin to recite "Om—nani—lali—rum" in time with your steps, so that the mantra is completed once for every eight steps you take (for musicians, this would be 4/8 time). You might say the mantra out loud for the first several cycles to establish the rhythm before internalizing the mantra and continuing with your normal exercise routine. Once you internalize the repetition of the mantra in rhythm with the activity, continue to vocalize the final syllable "rum" of each sequence. Keeping the final "rum" audible will help focus your attention on the mantra and make it easier to avoid losing the mantra altogether.

- During all mantra-exercises focus your attention on the mantra while remaining aware of your surroundings and environment, particularly as it relates to safety issues.

- Continue the mantra repetition until the exercise period is finished.

Using mantra-exercise can be a very effective way to combine multiple elements of an attentional training program (discussed in more detail in the final chapter), including concentration practice, fitness training, and conscious "unplugging" moments throughout the day.

10 MOVING INTO MINDFULNESS

"Mindfulness" is a term commonly used interchangeably with "meditation." However, in a stricter sense, this is not altogether accurate. Mindfulness itself is a way of being in the world, an attentiveness to the present moment of experience (which is one of the major areas of interest to the auditioning actor, as we have already discussed at length). Present-moment mindfulness is *cultivated* through the use of meditation practice, many forms of which you have already learned. But there is also a particular form of meditation practice called mindfulness that is especially good at cultivating mindful awareness.

The meditation practices we have been working with so far have all been based on concentrating the attention on a particular object, sensation, or process and holding or returning the attention to that single focus for a period of time. In technical terms, this type of practice is called "focused attention meditation" or "FAM." Mindfulness meditation practice goes a step further and concentrates the attention on the entire field of awareness as it arises in consciousness, holding no particular object as "center"; every sensation, thought, or even disturbance becomes the subject of attentional focus. Because of this "open awareness" or "bare attention" to all experience as it occurs in the present moment, we call mindfulness meditation "open monitoring meditation" or "OMM."

A variety of people and approaches to meditation training have a variety of viewpoints on this, but I think it is most useful to start attentional training by utilizing concentration techniques (FAM) first and then moving to mindfulness techniques (OMM) after some control over the basic attention function has been gained. Otherwise, it is very easy to get lost in the constant stream of ongoing experience without enough control to be able to focus the attention function on what is arising. Therefore, I am introducing actual mindfulness meditation exercises last.

Mindfulness Exercise

The basic instructions for the mindfulness exercise are identical to those for seated meditation practice in terms of no cellphones, quiet surroundings where you will not be interrupted, sitting/lying comfortably with eyes in a soft focus, etc.

Instructions:

- Take a moment to settle into your body. Release any tension and allow your awareness to focus on your breathing.

- Simply experience your body breathing for the next 5 breaths.

- As you breathe, continue to release any tension you may become aware of while you turn your attention inside.

- Now, let your awareness expand to include the sensations of your entire body. Become aware of any sensations, such as hot or cold, any tingling, or places of numbness, aches or pains. Whatever sensations are there, just acknowledge them; perhaps give them a

label: "Coolness. Numbness. Aching. Tingling."
Whatever is there. Just allow the sensations in your
body to enter your consciousness, label them, and
then gently let them go without judgment.

- And now, let your awareness expand to include your
sense of smell. Are there any subtle aromas in the
room around you? Can you smell your own cologne
or perfume? Body odor? Are there other scents in the
air? Just be with your sense of smell for a while and if
you identify a smell, simply label it, in a non-
judgmental way; and then let it go, as you continue to
inhabit this space at this moment.

- Now, let your awareness expand to include any
sounds you might hear in the room … the sound of
the air conditioner … the sound of the floor or the
walls creaking … the sound of your breathing …
sounds coming from outside of the room. Just take in
any sounds that happen to be present in this moment
and gently acknowledge them, perhaps give them a
label, and then let them go.

- And now, let your awareness expand to include the
entire room. Whatever sensations you might be
having in this room at this very moment, just be with
them for a moment. Be alive in this moment … in
this room. And any sensations or thoughts or feelings
that might arise, simply acknowledge them, perhaps
give them a one- or two-word label, and then let them
float on by with the next moment … which becomes
this present moment of time, with its unique sensory
and mental impressions. Just be here … be in the
now in this very moment, whatever it happens to
bring.

- If at any time you find your mind has wandered away
from your present awareness of the moment, gently

acknowledge the sensation, thought, memory, or emotion that has captured your attention, and let it go without judgment and allow your attention to return to this present moment in this very room.

- And now, slowly and gently, when you are ready, allow your awareness to re-inhabit your body and your breath. Take a few moments to simply breathe as you come back to the activity in the room and the rest of your day.

This is the basic mindfulness meditation practice, where any experience that arises, mental or physical sensation, momentarily becomes the object of attention before being gently acknowledged and then let go. It is consciousness becoming aware of itself in each successive present moment.

It may take some practice to let go of the various objects of attention, such as breath or other sensations, that you have been focusing on with such intensity in your earlier concentration practices, and simply let awareness be aware; but with time, mindfulness practice will become one of the most powerful exercises in your actor's toolkit.

With mindfulness practice, you should internalize the instructions as soon as is practical and make mindfulness meditation a main core practice that is entered into through the breath and then followed into each successive moment of the session. In core practice, the individual directions for mindfulness practice found in the scripted version are dropped and awareness is simply followed for awareness's sake: mindfully, in the moment, just so. Your very being will provide the content.

Informal Mindfulness Practices

Another very useful application of mindfulness (OMM) practice is to bring that same state of open awareness of experience rising to other activities in your life that you usually do mind*less*ly or without attention.

One of the most common activities of human beings is eating. In most cases, it is something we do several times a day and often under a variety of circumstances. In many cases, eating is done habitually with little awareness dedicated to the act or the sensations of the act beyond satisfying the overriding goal of quenching physical hunger. While an exquisite or special occasion meal may merit careful attention to the various flavors, smells and other pleasures of eating, most often, particularly in Western culture, we plow through our meals with little actual consciousness of the activity.

Below, I describe the process for applying informal mindfulness practice in the course of a daily meal.

Instructions:

- Prepare your meal and place it on a table or tray before you. Sit comfortably but erect. If you normally slouch at the dining table, you might consider sitting on the front edge of the chair with your body aligned and your back relatively straight as in a seated meditation posture. The idea is to be comfortable but alert throughout the dining experience without the need to shift or change positions often, so that the focus can remain on the act of eating.

- Take a few moments to settle into your seat and become present to the moment. You might bring your attention to the breath for a few cycles.

- Visually take in the food before you. Observe the colors of the food. Is there steam coming off any of the items? What aromas do you smell? Are there any sensations in your body as you gaze upon the meal you are about to partake of? Are you salivating? Is your stomach grumbling? Do you have the sensation of hunger? Take in the sounds of the room. Fully open yourself to your senses before you begin to eat. How does it feel just before you take your first bite of food?

- Slowly and mindfully pick up an eating utensil or piece of food, as appropriate. Experience the muscles in your arm and hand as you reach forward and grasp the item. If you have picked up a fork or spoon, explore it for a moment. Turn it over in your hand. What are its qualities? Weight? Does it sparkle in the light?

- If you have picked up a food item, explore it in the same way. What is the texture of the food? Does it bend? Is it spongy? Look at it from all angles. Can you discover anything about this food that you have never noticed before? Does it make a sound when held close to your ear? Perhaps touch it to your cheek or your lips without opening your mouth. What is the texture on your skin? Explore the item thoroughly before you begin eating.

- Check in with your body and your breath. Are there any sensations of anticipation? Take in the sounds and any activity in your surroundings. Be fully present to this moment just before placing food in your mouth.

- Place the first piece of food in your mouth, but do not begin chewing yet. Simply sense the food on your tongue. What is the temperature and texture? Is it juicy or dry? How does your body react to having food in the mouth and not chewing? What is the experience of taste before you begin to chew?

- If you used an eating utensil to place the food in your mouth, set it back down on the table and place your hands in your lap. Relax and bring your full attention to the act of beginning to chew the food. Chew slowly and deliberately. Try to experience each chewing motion as unique. Observe any changes in the sensations in your mouth as the bite of food is chewed. Experience the flavor as it is unlocked in the act of chewing. When it is time to swallow, do it deliberately. What is the sensation of swallowing like? Is the food swallowed all at once? Or is it done in a sequence? Finish the entire chewing and swallowing cycle before picking up your eating utensil and starting again.

- If it is time to take a drink of a beverage, bring the same level of mindfulness to the activity as you did with the food. Note the muscular mechanics of picking up the glass, the sensations before opening your mouth to take a sip, the sensations in your mouth as you take in the liquid, the flavors and sense of wetness on your tongue, and finally the swallowing of the beverage. Finish each drink completely and fully before moving on to the next.

- Continue the meal in this fashion until you are full and the meal has been completed.

Mindful eating, and other mindful awareness exercises similar to it, can be combined with a disciplined regime of formal attentional training exercises to extend and leverage your mindful moments throughout the day, taking full advantage of the cumulative qualities of meditation practice.

Many people will initially claim they have little time in their rushed daily schedules for regular attentional training; however, by carefully using a menu of informal mindful exercises combined with more formal FAM and OMM work as described earlier, sometimes in short intervals at multiple times during the day, a significant attention training program can be executed with very little schedule disruption or change. As with anything of significance, the importance imbued upon the work itself and the intention with which it is engaged will often determine its actual viability more than a cursory and superficial dismissal.

Now that I have introduced you to several types of attentional training exercises, both focused attentions and open monitoring (or mindfulness), it is time to look at how you can design a personal program for yourself, using these tools to improve your attention, reduce nerves, and bring you into the present moment of every audition you have during your career. But first, I want to introduce a different type of exercise I call "intentional" and that focuses on our perceptions of "self" in a slightly different but useful way.

11 INTERLUDE THREE: PSYCHOLOGY AND SELF-CONFIDENCE

At this point, I would like to introduce a totally different kind of exercise to your training regimen called *intentional* training, which instead of training the attention function directly, focuses more on our internal self-image and how we relate to our sense of self. For this chapter, instead of relying on meditation techniques, I will use the tools of modern psychology to explore ways to improve self-confidence and "presence" while in the audition situation.

Many actors think of psychology as simply the investigation of character motivation, but this is a very limited viewpoint. (For a detailed exploration of how psychology from various schools can be used by the actor, see my upcoming book: *Psychology for Actors*, Routledge Press, Fall 2018.)

There is an entire field of psychology dedicated to the study and understanding of happy emotions, self-esteem, and mental wellbeing, called "positive psychology." One of the most interesting areas of research in positive psychology, at least as far as working actors are concerned, is the study of self-confidence and the sensation of personal empowerment (or its reverse: powerlessness) and how that affects individual competence in high-pressure situations (such as in the audition room). It turns out that our attitude about ourselves, and even the way we bear our bodies, can have significant impacts on how well we present ourselves to others in an audition. And, just like the attention function, a sense of personal power can be cultivated and enhanced by certain exercises that I will describe later in this chapter.

Because what I will be describing below does not directly work on the attention function (although it will certainly have an impact on how efficient your focus of attention is likely to be), I will call this part of the training "intentional" exercises so as to make them distinct from the "attentional" exercises we have already learned. In the final chapter, I will put both kinds of training together in an outline of a year-long program for improving both your audition success and your work as an actor during live or filmed performances.

In 2012, Amy Cuddy, a Harvard professor of social psychology, gave one of the most viewed TED Talks in history. This talk was entitled "Your Body Language May Shape Who You Are" and has now been viewed more than 44 million times! After the success of her TED Talk, Cuddy published a book, *Presence: Bringing Your Boldest Self to Your Biggest Challenges* (Little Brown, 2015) that I recommend to all actors who audition for a living. I will briefly discuss Cuddy's work (and others below); but to really get the full impact and the why of how Cuddy's work is important to the actor, you really should read her book cover to cover.

Dr. Cuddy believes that people, and this of course would extend to actors, do their best and most authentic work in high-pressure situations (particularly those where we are representing ourselves to others, such as during job interviews, public speeches, or acting auditions) when they have a strong sense of *personal power*. She delineates between *social power*, which is the ability to influence others, and personal power, the ability to control our own internal emotional states and behaviors, and points out how feeling *powerless* can have all sorts of negative impacts on how well we present ourselves in these kinds of situations. So, you can see that if an audition situation is about presenting yourself and your acting talents for a particular role, then having some control over your own confidence and sense of personal power can be, and often is, the critical deciding factor between success and failure!

One of Cuddy's more amazing discoveries is that physical posturing can actually affect, in a significant way, your individual sense of personal empowerment. The fact that certain types of physicalization or movement can alter one's emotional state and expression has been well known to actors, on an intuitive level at least, for centuries. But what Cuddy has done is use science and the modern experimental method to demonstrate this fact.

The Power Pose

I was first introduced to using power posing as a way to prepare for acting challenges (or auditioning) by assistant professor of theatre Neal Utterback, who teaches undergraduate actors at Juniata College in Huntingdon, Pennsylvania. Neal has created a unique set of exercises for his young actors that includes certain types of meditation practice, high-intensity exercise training, mental imagery and self-talk regimens, and a technique based on Cuddy's work, called "Olympic Power Posing." My approach for improving auditioning is slightly different and simplified from Utterback's work, yet still attempts to exert a similar influence on self-confidence and "presence" in the moment.

Back to Amy Cuddy, she and a group of researches devised several experiments to identify both the physiological and psychological impacts of physical posturing on self-image and confidence. Based on the observation that animals in nature, when faced with conflict or danger, will often adopt an expansive posture that fills up more space and makes the animal look larger (and perhaps more threatening) to a predator, Cuddy's team studied the differences between human postures that were either expansive and dominant, perhaps even aggressive, and those that were more closed off and constricted, such as slouching or curling up into a ball.

According the Cuddy's research reports, her science team was able to identify higher levels of testosterone (a hormone associated with aggression and dominance) and lower levels of cortisol (a hormone that is released when a person is under high levels of stress) in subjects that adopted powerful or strong/expansive physical poses for relatively short periods of time (two to five minutes) than in subjects who adopted more "subservient" or constricted physical postures.

To be fair, I need to point out that this research remains somewhat controversial and several aspects of the initial reports have failed to be replicated by other researchers; however, the subjective, psychological reports of the experimental subjects remain valid: The power posers felt more confident, self-assured, and personally empowered. In other words, even if the science behind the physiological effects that Cuddy's team first reported remains dubious, how the subjects responded psychologically to the power-posing exercises correlates perfectly with the way we want to present ourselves as actors: with a cool, calm, and self-possessed presence under pressure. As one actor to another: wouldn't you pay money for a technique that you could use intentionally to make yourself feel more powerful and in control right before you walked into an important audition?

Yes. I Am. Great!

The following exercise can be done in conjunction with your daily attentional training and also as a warm-up (perhaps in the bathroom or private corner) before stepping into an audition room. This exercise is great for calming nerves, focusing attention, and reinforcing a feeling of strength and confidence in a high-pressure situation.

Instructions:

- Stand with feet shoulder-width apart and hands relaxed at your sides. Take a few deep, centering breaths before you begin and bring your attention into the present moment. Take a few moments to scan your body for tensions and let those go.

- Take two large, bold steps in any direction, ending with feet planted firmly, and spread your arms wide to both sides in front of you (as if you are inviting a huge bear-hug).

- In a firm, confident voice proclaim, "Yes!"

- From this position of welcoming the world, repeat the activity by taking another two steps in any direction, swinging the arms freely, and end again with feet planted firmly, still at shoulder-width apart, spreading your arms wide and proclaiming "Yes!"

- Repeat for two minutes, making each move intentional and each proclamation bold and confident.

- Concentrate on your feeling of personal power and groundedness. Personalize each "Yes!" so that it becomes an affirmation of yourself in this moment; let it become something joyous, an exciting agreement with the universe.

- When you feel it is time, change to the next movement by taking two firm steps in any direction, this time planting your fists on your hips and thrusting your chest up and forward (this is sometimes called the "Wonder Woman Pose"), and proclaim in a full powerful voice, "I Am!"

- As before, repeat this move for approximately two

minutes, allowing your proclamations to evolve and become more personal with each iteration.

- When you feel it is time, change to the next movement by taking two firm steps in any direction, this time throwing your arms out above your head in a V shape, hands flat like blades and fingers extended towards the sky (this is often called the "Victory Pose"), and call out "Great!"

- Repeat as before for two minutes, making each move intentional and each proclamation bold and confident.

- Finally, combine all three movements into a series and perform for two more minutes: two steps in any direction, arms open wide as if to hug the world, "Yes!" Two more steps, fists on hips, chest thrust forward, "I Am!" Two steps, arms high in the air in a V, "Great!"

If this exercise is properly embodied and you give yourself over to it fully while embracing a "super hero" type of boldness and even brashness, you will find that this short 8-minute exercise can significantly pump you up and "get your adrenaline going" (in the right kind of way). Generally speaking, particularly if you are subject to nervousness, shaky hands, or shortness of breath before an audition, this single exercise can ground you and get you focused while eliminating the jitters altogether.

Sports Psychology and Preventing "The Choke"

Sian Beilock is an associate professor of psychology at the University of Chicago. She holds two PhDs, in kinesiology and psychology, and her research focuses on understanding what makes otherwise great athletes (and other high performers, like actors) fail to perform at their maximum potential (or even flub up badly) under certain high pressure situations. In the vernacular, this sometimes spectacular under-performance is called "choking" and is a well-known phenomenon in the sports world.

For actors, choking is the equivalent of succumbing to stage fright or "freezing up" during a scene or monologue that you otherwise have well memorized and have rehearsed many times. Choking during an audition is sometimes known as "the actor's nightmare," where you may have waited months or even years for "your big break" only to enter the audition room, stand before an important director, and completely forget the lines or become suddenly incapable of cold-reading up to your potential. We have all had fears of this happening; and if you've been in the business long enough, you've certainly experienced it for yourself more than once (see the story of my commercial spokesman audition in Chapter Three).

Dr. Beilock has not only studied the phenomenon of choking under pressure but also used neuroscience to reveal potential solutions to the problem. Once again, wouldn't you pay good money to insure against choking during your next big audition? I sure would!

Beilock's research showed that high-pressure environments (such as kicking a field goal in a professional football game, putting to win a golf championship, or auditioning for a Hollywood movie) induce a predictable set of physiological and mental states that include increased heart rate, a rush of adrenaline (in the negative sense, such as with anxiety), and cluttered or racing thoughts (often focused on worry about the outcome of the situation). Interestingly, when people worry about outcomes in high-pressure situations, they often try to control or repress the anxiety that comes along with that worry, leading to an even higher likelihood of choking when it really counts!

Basically, worry tends to highjack the prefrontal cortex, the part of your brain responsible for higher forms of reasoning and self-control (the exact kinds of mental functions most important during an acting audition), and make it more difficult to function in an intuitive and flowing manner. Essentially, if you are worried about the outcome of the audition situation (which is focusing on the future instead of the present moment), you are less likely to have the kind of mental control to help you perform well during that very same audition. Failure becomes a self-fulfilling prophecy.

To counteract the negative effects of worry during high-pressure situations, Beilock identified several activities that seem to be effective at both calming the nerves and bringing the athlete or performer more into the flow of the present moment (our same goals as actors). One of her main recommendations, not surprisingly, is meditation practice. But she also details some other practices of great value to the actor, which I describe below.

The following exercises can be done on a regular or recurring basis as general confidence-builders, and should be repeated, when possible, for at least a few minutes in the morning before your audition day begins.

Intentional Writing Exercises

In the course of her own research and in the study of other researchers' work, Beilock identified several activities involving short writing assignments that seem to help reduce the kinds of internal tensions that lead to choking under pressure. Below, I offer three of these practices that I have found particularly applicable to the audition situation.

Instructions:

> • Using a journal or private computer file that you can easily access (if you want to be able to do these exercises on the fly or immediately before entering the audition room; a small pocket journal may be preferable), do the following exercises before your audition.

- *Affirm your self-worth* by jotting down a list, or write a few short paragraphs, about your very best qualities as a human being. These do not need to be acting related, but rather your finest qualities, talents, and gifts that make you special, unique, and lovable as a person. This is purely a self-worth exercise and should be done with honesty and candor. If this is difficult for you, practice it until you can genuinely create a list that you can feel proud of. If you cannot come up with a list of truly positive qualities about yourself, even after much effort, you might want to see a psychologist or counselor to work on your deepest self-esteem issues.

- *Map your personal complexities* in a diagram format. Try to chart as many different aspects of your personality as you can. Look at all the roles you play in life (that are not related to your acting work) to uncover the richness of your unique and individual spirit. This kind of self-evaluation usually will put the audition process into a context that is less overwhelming and helps highlight your broader value as a human being (once again, helping to increase confidence and lessen nerves in the moment).

- *Describe your greatest fears about the audition* before you go in. This may seem counter-intuitive, but research has shown this type of work to be very helpful. Often fear and worry become amorphous or ill-defined and generalized. Therefore, in this exercise, write several paragraphs describing exactly what your fears are and articulate, in detail, the worst-case scenario you can imagine happening during your audition. Once you name those fears and "bring them into the light" they will tend to dissipate (not necessarily disappear, but become much weaker) and this will allow you to go ahead with the more positive feelings of self-worth generated in the first two exercises.

• If you like, you can start with this exercise first and then move to the other, more positive practices right before you go into the audition room.

This kind of work takes some courage and self-honesty; but when properly applied in conjunction with the power-posing exercises described before, it can create a potent "cocktail of confidence" for the actor who is meeting a significant personal challenge (such as a professional audition). Remember what Richard Feldman of the Julliard School said in Chapter Three: "There has to be a level of conscious awareness about your instrument [as an actor] that a regular person doesn't have to have." And that conscious awareness includes cultivating a purposeful and intentional sense of self-confidence that won't crack under pressure.

While meditation and attentional training exercises can help to calm nerves and cultivate a personal sense of presence in the moment, these types of intentional psychological exercises, particularly when repeated over time, provide an essential sense of self-confidence and self-value that is indispensable to the actor. Use both types of training regularly if you want to improve your results at winning acting work in a competitive situation.

12 A PERSONAL PROGRAM FOR
BETTER AUDITIONS

At this point, I have presented to you with several different ways you can go about training your attention function and intentional "prescence", and research has indicated that certain benefits will accrue if that training is sustained over a period of time. So as an actor, how do you apply what you have learned so far? In particular, how do you apply this work to the audition situation?

Using attentional (meditation) and intentional training to improve your performance and presence in the audition room needs to be approached in two distinct ways, each dependent on the other. You, therefore, will need to apply what you have learned in both ways to gain the full effect. Some of the benefits occur automatically after you have been practicing a disciplined program regularly over time. Once you have established that practice, you can use specific exercises before, during, and after the audition session to amplify and perfect the technical delivery of the audition performance. I will cover both applications of attentional and intentional training below, starting with how to custom develop a daily practice, followed by a series of exercises you can do on the day of your audition. I promise that if you diligently practice both approaches to deploying and utilizing your attention function, the impact on your auditions will noticeably improve!

A One-Year Program of Daily Attentional Training

Here's the bottom line: Attentional training takes a similar level of self-discipline as does vocal training, movement training, or acting class. It is an *applied* training, meaning that the benefits are in direct proportion to the actual time spent doing the activity and those benefits have little to do with reading about or intellectually understanding the processes involved. You either do the training, or you don't.

In truth, less than half of the people who read this book will actually do the work required. While I have no statistical data to back up that claim, I do have years of experience as both an actor and a meditator and so my guess here is at least well educated. I will also point out that 50% of the people who read this book will give up the acting profession within a year of going "pro." Those are simply the statistics for the industry. But those who do stick it out and succeed professionally almost always engage in ongoing self-training and self-improvement of one form or another.

If you are among those who take your career as an actor seriously and plan to be as prepared as you can be for the challenges that lie ahead, I present the following outline of an attentional/intentional training program. If you follow the instructions, adapting the program to your own lifestyle and schedule so that you stick to it for the full year, your auditioning and acting performances will improve.

Here are some important concepts to keep in mind as you begin your training in earnest:

- Attentional training is *cumulative*; the more you do it, the better you get at it.

- Attentional training is *progressive*; the benefits grow in impact the longer you are engaged in the practice (the ways you improve after a month may well be different from the ways you improve after a year).

- Attentional training can be either *formal* (such as seated meditation practice) or *informal* (mindful eating, for instance), but the formal practice is what makes informal practice effective. In other words, you should probably start with formal practice and then move into informal practice as you become more skillful at placing your attention, rather than the other way around.

- Everyone *progresses differently* and at one's own pace through attentional training, so the following are guidelines only. The program you develop for yourself should be one that you can follow regularly as an integrated part of your lifestyle. A program that you don't actually do is of little use to you as an actor (or as a human being).

The program outline I present below is very basic; it is at the beginner's level and not intended to be a complete course in consciousness training. If you like this training and it provides benefits for you, I encourage you to seek out a formal meditation teacher to help guide you through more advanced training. Serious meditation training (meaning hours a day and regular extended retreats) should only be undertaken under the guidance of an experienced teacher. But, for now, you can begin here. If you are interested in scientific studies that underlie this work, please see my forthcoming book, *Advanced Consciousness Training (A.C.T.) for Actors*, available starting in September of 2018 from Routledge Press. *A.C.T. for Actors* is aimed at the conservatory actor who is going through three to four years of extensive training under the supervision of seasoned master acting teachers and thus goes into far greater detail than I am able to do in this introductory book on auditioning.

The following program outline is based on a year of regular formal attentional training. I will discuss specific informal exercises that can be done for auditions in a later section.

The First Two Months

The first two months of your attentional training program are about exploring the various exercises you have learned in previous chapters and learning what does and does not work well for you. You are encouraged to try each form of attention exercise for at least 10 days so that you can gain a true feel for each one.

Your initial goal will be to do some form of daily practice for between 15 and 20 minutes. This is considered to be about the minimum threshold of attentional training that will, in the early phases, help people improve their powers of concentration. If you miss a session, don't worry or engage in self-judgment, simply return to the practice the next day and continue on. While your target is every day for the first two months, if you manage to get in five sessions a week, you are doing great!

You can include, in some of your 10-day cycles, experiments with apps such as Headspace and Calm (see Chapter Six for more on these types of mobile apps); but primarily it's effective to experience the various forms of concentration meditation (counting breaths, body-scan, walking meditation, mantra, etc.).

Your main task or goal in these first two months is to develop a daily habit of attentional training, to get comfortable with the idea of working your "attentional muscles" on a regular basis.

Months Two Through Four

Once you have become familiar with the various exercises and established a daily habit, you will begin to formalize (and deepen) your practice by focusing on one form of concentration meditation for the next two months. This will allow you to start to work directly on your powers of focused attention.

Choose one of the seated meditation techniques, either counting breaths or mantra, and focus on that exercise for 20 minutes a day for the next two months. Remember that one of the main purposes of these exercises is to practice noticing when you become distracted (which is inevitable) and gently return your awareness to the object of concentration. This process of non-judgmentally reorienting your attention over and over again is the key to all of the benefits of attentional training; so don't get frustrated (particularly at this early stage), but welcome the chance to identify distraction and gently but firmly refocus. Eventually, this single activity will extend itself into all other areas of your life and become a powerful tool in your actor's toolkit.

During this period, do not change exercises. Stick with either counting breaths or repeating a mantra for the entire time, even if progress seems slow or frustrating. The purpose of this period is to begin training the attention function to your will, and it turns out that a variety of activities is not as useful as discipline to a single activity at this point. Don't worry, you will have a chance to vary your exercises at a later stage of training. For now, be brave and diligent.

One thing that can be useful in establishing a daily attentional training practice is to prepare a quiet, dedicated area for your practice sessions. Perhaps it is your living room couch? Or maybe a chair in the corner of your bedroom? Some people like to meditate on a cushion or bench on their porch or other peaceful outside area where they won't be interrupted (but do be cautious about selecting environments where there are a number of built-in distractions, such as traffic noise or pedestrian traffic or anywhere you may be approached by people who might want to talk to you). The rule of thumb is to select a spot where you feel comfortable and safe while concentrating deeply on your internal landscape for at least the 20 minutes of your session.

Make this space a special spot for yourself, a place where you go specifically to meditate. By establishing a distinct location for your daily meditation practice, you also establish the habit, when inhabiting that space, of taking the activity seriously and entering a quiet, introspective state every time you sit there. Having a dedicated meditation space is part of setting the proper intention to take this work seriously.

Months Five Through Eight

Now that you have established a regular daily meditation practice, it is time to deepen the work even further.

If you have been counting breaths, it is time to drop the internal counting and simply follow the sensation of breathing in and out during your meditation sessions. This transition from conscious counting to following sensation with bare attention may be difficult for some. At first it may seem like breaking a habit (because it is!). However, after a couple of days, it should become easier to attend only to the sensation of the breath. If you are still finding it difficult to maintain your attention on the breath after a week, you may return to counting, but take care not to use the counting as a crutch or a distraction from focusing on pure experience; the counting part of this exercise is only to help you initially focus your attention and eventually will become a distraction itself.

If you have been chanting a mantra out loud, it is time to fully internalize the mantra by repeating it silently "in your head" and avoid even mouthing the words so that your attention becomes fully focused on the repetition of the sounds and not the mechanics of the words in your mouth. If you have already been using the mantra silently, you might try dropping the mantra in favor of following the sensation of breath as recommended above.

The point of this type of attentional training is to begin focusing on the subtler elements of the object of attention and to winnow away any excess movements or embellishments so that only the object (in most cases the breath) remains in consciousness. The more still you can sit during your sessions, the deeper your ability to focus your attention function will become.

In addition to the heightened focus of attention during this phase, you can also start to add both time to your sessions (30 minutes per day will be your goal now) and some of the informal practices described in previous chapters, like mindful eating (see Chapter Ten). This lengthening of training time can be accomplished in several ways. You can simply extend the length of your daily formal practice session by 10 minutes. You can also add 10 minutes of Walking Meditation to whatever version of seated meditation you have adopted. Or, you can split your daily session into two 15 minutes sessions, one in the morning and one in the evening.

As long as you ramp up your formal meditation time to 30 minutes every day, you will find that your once dancing, busy thoughts will start to calm down and it will become easier to direct and hold your attention on an object, both during your sessions and during the rest of your day—including at auditions.

During this phase of training, try adding at least one informal practice three times a week. This could include eating a mindful meal, taking a mindful shower or bath, mindfully washing the dishes or sweeping the floor. Almost any activity that you do in daily life can become a mindfulness exercise by bringing your full attention to the experience. Many actors find informal practice pleasant, even amusing, and become quite creative at finding activities to "do mindfully."

One word of caution. Do not attempt to utilize mindfulness training techniques with activities that could be potentially dangerous, such as driving a car or working with heavy equipment. While the goal of mindfulness training is to be fully present to the experiential details of an activity, the turning inward of attention with great focus can still act as a distraction to activities that require speed and manual dexterity, so do use your common sense.

Months Nine Through Twelve

By this point in your training, if you have been diligent and regular with your sessions, you will have seen noticeable improvements in your attention function. It is now time to turn from your concentration exercises to the open monitoring style of meditation practice, where your attention is opened to all experience as it arises.

As described in Chapter Ten, OMM exercises drop all counting and mantras in favor of simply being aware of your experience while sitting completely still during the session. All experience becomes the object of attention. This can include physical sensations, sensory input like sounds and smells, as well as thoughts, emotions, and memories. The goal during an OMM session is to identify whatever happens to enter awareness and then let it go without judgment or attachment. This sounds simple but can actually be quite challenging at first. This is why we spent the first nine months of our training regimen working on improving concentration of attention before moving to OMM.

You may want to begin this phase of your training by returning to the guided version of this meditation. As before, there are guided recordings of many forms of mindfulness meditation available for free on the Internet, and you can go to my website for a version based on this book to get you started. However, once you have mastered the instructions and become comfortable with OMM, it is usually best to do the session in complete silence and sit very still. That way it is easier to identify subtle movements or external sounds as they arise in awareness and make them, for just a moment, the object of attention before gently and easily letting them go.

One other variation on the training during this period is to alternate sessions of concentration on breath or mantra with OMM sessions, usually one in the morning and one in the afternoon. The point remains to practice at least 30 minutes each day so that you gain a stronger, more concrete control of your attention function.

By Month Nine, you will probably be ready to attempt a silent retreat (described in the next section), which can be a wholly different kind of experience from a daily formal and informal practice.

By the end of this year-long program, if you have practiced the suggested amount of time every day, you will have directly trained your attention function for approximately 160 hours. Your ability to focus will be noticeably improved. You will probably be less nervous and more confident in general. And your capacity to listen and respond spontaneously (in the moment) will be noticeably better. In other words, by simply doing the training described in this book once or twice a day for short periods, you will have already gained the benefits I promised at the start of this book without any additional effort. Anyone who has ever learned to sing, dance, play a musical instrument, or master some other kind of specialty skill that is important to their art will immediately recognize that this is a very small time commitment for a potentially huge gain. (160 hours is less time than you would spend on a single play when you add up audition preparation time, rehearsal, and performance hours.)

In the final sections of this chapter, I will describe some additional exercises and experiences that will help you directly with the audition situation.

The Silent Retreat

A very powerful training tool utilized by many

established meditation traditions is the silent retreat. A silent retreat is an extended period of time, usually running anywhere from half a day to as many as ten days (or longer), where participants set aside the concerns of their daily lives and focus intensely, and exclusively, on group and individual meditation practice. A three-day silent retreat is very common, particularly for relative beginners, and will be the model I base this discussion on. The retreat takes place at an off-site retreat center where all of the participants' basic needs are taken care of, such as food and simple sleeping accommodations.

A silent retreat offers many unique opportunities and experiences for personal growth and the deepening of an individual meditation practice. For one thing, most people are not used to being around others for extended periods of silence. During the retreat, participants are encouraged to remain in complete vocal silence for the entire time and to avoid even non-verbal communication or eye contact with other participants in order to concentrate on their inner experiences without distraction or the responsibility of communication.

During the course of the retreat, the exclusive focus is on engagement with various forms of meditative practice and a constant cultivation of bare attention, or mindfulness, in all activities, including walking and eating. There is no music and no reading during the retreat period. No mobile technology, phone calls, or television are allowed. During break periods, participants are encouraged to remain mindful at all times and often, depending on the environment of the retreat center, they can walk in nature or do necessary chores, such as sweeping the floors or cleaning the dishes by hand. Meditation sessions are scheduled throughout the day and evening, often beginning very early, with pre-breakfast sessions starting at 6:00 a.m. Meditation practice usually alternates between seated sessions (which may be either FAM or OMM-oriented) and walking or other forms of movement meditation and sometimes yoga. Breaks are taken for meals as needed.

Sometimes there are private sessions with the retreat leader or on-site meditation teacher to discuss individual experience and ask questions. These sessions (in Zen practice called dokusan) are held in private so as not to disturb the other participants and are the only exception to the rule of silence during the course of the retreat.

Extended silent retreats can significantly increase the intensity of attentional training practice and are much more likely to produce noticeable altered states of consciousness than normal short doses of daily practice. These altered states can be very powerful and moving experiences that can lead to personal insights and even life-changing revelations. It is highly recommended that if you engage in a silent retreat, a qualified meditation teacher be on site and involved for the entire retreat period. A silent retreat is a serious endeavor and should not be attempted without supervision.

There are numerous retreat centers around the country, often accessible in your local area, with many other options available if you are willing to travel. These centers offer structured retreats based on various forms or styles of meditative practice. Mindfulness retreats (sometimes called vipassanā) are very popular and widely available. Make sure to do your research and only commit to reputable programs run by established centers with good records. You want to feel comfortable and supported in the retreat setting, and having confidence in the teacher or retreat leader is very important for cultivating the proper state of mind to release yourself wholly to the experience.

Also, by this point in your training, it is highly recommended that you seek out an established meditation group for support. Going much beyond this introductory level of training definitely requires a qualified teacher, so do some research on what is available in your local area and find someone who can support and teach you more about the practice than you can learn in a book. Not everything that comes up on a meditation cushion is pleasant, and a good teacher is a must for advanced practice and to answer the hard questions that sometimes emerge from deep introspection.

The potential power of a silent retreat experience is difficult to describe in written form and generally must be experienced to be appreciated.

Audition-specific Attentional Exercises

So far, I have presented my program of attentional training in a fairly linear fashion. However, this is not necessarily how you will actually engage this work "in real life." For instance, you may certainly use the following tactics and strategies for improving your audition success well before you complete the year-long course of formal training described at the beginning of this chapter; I would expect you to. The following exercises will simply work better after you have begun to reign some control over your attention function.

The truth is, all of the exercises I have proposed will become more effective with practice, so use them all, use them regularly, and use them with discipline for greatest effect. And, once you "get good at it," plan on finding a qualified teacher and joining a group to work with to advance your skills. In reality, those are pretty simple instructions for a program that can literally change your artistic and personal life! Remember, the initial work only asks for 160 hours over the course of a year.

Confidence Repetitions

To begin with, definitely plan to start using the power posing ("Yes. I am. Great!" exercise) and the intentional writing exercises presented in the last chapter, right away. These can help with a personal sense of confidence and embodied presence with almost no long-term practice before hand; they just work.

As early as the end of your first month of training, you can begin to use one, or a combination of several, of the following exercises actually at (or immediately before) an audition session to cultivate and reinforce the three important qualities that you are trying to train with this work: concentration of attention, relaxation under pressure, and being present in the moment.

The Three-Breaths Centering Exercise

Remember that I have said that this training is both *cumulative* and *progressive*; meaning the more you do the formal practices, the easier it becomes to access the positive effects in informal settings. So, once you have begun to experience the calming of thoughts, the lessening of tension, and the bringing of your attention function to heel, all of which accompany this type of consciousness training, it becomes a fairly simple matter to "remind your brain" how to come to attention at will. (If you are interested in the neuroscientific explanations of why that is so, see my book, *Advanced Consciousness Training for Actors,* coming from Routledge in the Fall of 2018.)

Instructions:

While waiting in the office or lobby of the audition location, find a chair (or even an unoccupied corner) where you can focus inward for a few moments.

Sit with a relatively straight back (or find a "centered position" if standing) and turn your attention inward for a moment, simply ignoring any distractions in the room. (Do you see why this might get easier after some extended home practice?)

You can close your eyes or, if it seems more socially appropriate to the situation, pretend to be intently reading over your sides and working on your lines (most actors will do you the courtesy of leaving you alone if they think you are preparing).

Focus your attention on the sensation of the breath entering and leaving your body, just as in your formal meditation practice, for three full breath cycles. If you have the time, take the exercise all the way up to 10 breaths. (Note that this exercise is equally effective for mantra meditators.)

It is that simple. Because you have been training your mind to calm and focus regularly during your home practice, this simple and short reminder to your brain that it is time to come to attention can be miraculously effective. I use this technique before every audition and it nearly always works to immediately calm my nerves and bring my focus into the room and the task at hand. Why do I say "nearly"? Because everyone has a bad day sometimes. Again, see my story of the commercial spokesman audition in Chapter Three. (And remember that I had been doing this kind of work for 35+ years and meditate every day!)

This exercise can easily be done in your parked car before you walk into the audition location, or on public transportation if that is how you travel. The important thing to remember is to physically *do* the exercise; by enacting all of the formal steps of a meditation session (sitting calmly, turning the awareness inward, focusing on the breath, etc.), you will literally activate the neuronal pathways in your brain that have become conditioned by repeated practice (scientists have found evidence that repeated behavior actually alters the physical structures of our brains).

The Pacing Cheat

Many actors will pace the waiting room before being called into the audition (usually memorizing their lines or attempting to cultivate their own concentration). You can use this professionally accepted behavior to your advantage: become a pacer! Only, in your case, pace in a mindful manner just as in the Walking Meditation exercise introduced earlier.

See Chapter Eight for the instructions.

Mindful of the Room Exercise

Once you have progressed to using open monitoring meditation or mindfulness practice (introduced in Chapter Ten), you can bring mindfulness meditation with you into the audition waiting room as a way to directly stimulate present moment awareness.

By the time you have progressed to using mindfulness practice as part of your daily training routine, you will probably have gotten pretty good at the basics of training your attention function so that what I will suggest below may simply occur naturally. However, for convenience sake, I will include some condensed instructions below:

Wherever you are located in the room, turn your attention inward, release any physical tensions you find in the body, and focus on your breath for a few cycles (this will help to focus your attention at the beginning).

Close your eyes, if appropriate, or you can use the "I'm learning my lines by looking at my script" body posture described in the Three-Breaths Centering Exercise above.

Let your awareness expand to include your entire body and note any sensations you happen to find there (releasing any tensions that you are able to).

After a few moments, let your awareness expand to your senses of smell, hearing, etcetera. Simply make note of each sensory input as it arises, perhaps label it, and then let it go without judgment.

When it seems appropriate, let your awareness expand to include the entire room, the sounds of the other actors, the various conversations, the fluorescent lighting, your own thoughts, feelings, and emotions (even the thoughts, feelings, and emotions of the character for which you are preparing?); whatever arises in your awareness, acknowledge it, label it, and let it go. Allow your awareness to be open to and present with whatever experience there is in this present moment.

If you find that your attention has become distracted, perhaps by a specific conversation or other activity in the room, simply acknowledge the distraction as an event in consciousness, and let that go, too, returning your attention to the next thing that arises in the present moment.

Continue this for five minutes (if the situation allows).

Five minutes of purposeful mindfulness practice in the audition waiting room before you go in can literally work miracles for your attention, nerves, and presence. By the time you reach this level of attentional training, you will already be well aware of the benefits of this type of exercise and will be doing this automatically without any prompting from a book. You will already be 150% better at auditioning!

Conclusion: Diamonds and Pudding

I once had a mentor, the great American psychologist and consciousness researcher, Dr. James Fadiman, who taught me the idea of the "diamonds and pudding universe." This will be a terrible condensation of Dr. Fadiman's ideas, but I will attempt to relate it to the work I have introduced for the auditioning actor in this book.

Fadiman suggested that the entire substance of the universe (all being, all time, all everything) is essentially like a soft, creamy pudding: malleable and shapeable from a certain viewpoint; not predetermined but evolving. And, within that endless universe of relatively soft pudding, human thoughts and intentions are like diamonds: hard, solid, and with dense substance (at least relative to the pudding make-up of everything else).

And so, if we have a thought, a goal, or an intention to proceed down a certain path in life, that is something like plunging a hard diamond into the pudding of the universe: the universe yields to our focused intentions, it forms around the diamonds of our thoughts and emotions, offering support from every angle instead of resistance. Thoughts are harder than what we normally think of as objective "reality."

I always thought that was a nice metaphor for describing how life could be lived, with a positive outlook towards the universe and our individual agency as human beings within it. Our thoughts are like diamonds forming the universe of pudding around us. Cool!

To extend that idea just a little further, the techniques I have shown you in this book are like the jeweler's tools in that pudding universe, capable (when wielded by a skilled hand) of taking a rough chunk of diamond rock and transforming it into a beautiful and multifaceted jewel of great value.

Mindfulness and attentional training for an actor is a very powerful way to shape the universe around us. And as performers of any ilk, the substance of our thoughts are really about the only thing of true value we bring to the table when we audition (or when we get the job). It is our calling to refine and hone our thoughts, intentions, and attentional skills to their highest and brightest potential, like diamonds in a universe of sweet, soft pudding. By polishing "our diamond" (which really is our talent), we enter the universe around us on new terms, more powerful and embodied terms, that allow us to sculpt the present moment when we step across the threshold into the audition space in ways that are more intentional, bold, and creative; we become better at what we do as actors.

Be a diamond …

13 BONUSES FROM THE BLOG

Over the years, I have published several blogs on various subjects that interest me (and, hopefully, other people). Nowadays, I am most prolific when it comes to discussing the theories and practicalities of the actor's life. The short articles I write for www.KevinPage.com cover a much wider variety of subject matters than just mindfulness practices applied to the auditioning situation.

Below is a sample of short writings that I have posted about the acting life, along with an invitation to become a member of my blog and share its existence with other actors if you find the information informative and useful (or even entertaining). Enjoy!

A Financial-STYLE Model for Creative Time

In my professional life, I have worn a number of hats. I am what you call a serial creative. I have mostly been engaged in traditional "artistic" fields (like acting, writing and painting), but have also spent time in areas considered more "traditional" (like stock broking and investment banking).

Regardless of the field, I've always managed to leave my

own mark on whatever I was doing, an indication of serial creativity in action, I suppose.

One of my jobs over the years was to prepare and deliver financial plans to individual investors who wanted to both protect and grow their retirement savings. To do this, I would usually propose a portfolio that was diversified across several asset classes (stocks, bonds, commodities, real estate, etc.). The reason for this, at least theoretically, is to control risk. If you have your money spread out in a lot of different places, you not only have a lot of ways to make money, you also have a lot of ways to avoid losing money when markets become volatile (as they always eventually do).

So, several years ago I charted out my multifarious career paths on a piece of paper. I noticed that, in many ways, it looked like one of these investment portfolios that I used to recommend. Some of my pursuits have been successful, but there have also been long stretches of time filled with work that ultimately led to a dead end. For instance, actors can audition for months and not get a paying job.

The fact that I have had a mix of activities over the years has really helped to even out the financial volatility that is perhaps more common in arts careers than in most other fields. And so, I had a very simple idea: If you are an artist (of any type) or aspire to be one, why not plan your path to success in the same general way that you would purposefully build a retirement portfolio?

Plan to diversify your assets (time/creativity) across multiple investments (what you want to do with your talent): acting, writing, art, etc., and spread it across different kinds of investments. (An actor, for instance, may audition for films and TV but also do commercials or voice overs, possibly print modeling, theater, and such.) See my article: "Diversifying Your Artistic Portfolio" for a more complete discussion of this idea.

Here's an example from IMDB.COM. It's what I like to

call: "Stock Charts for Acting Careers."

IMDB.com is the main professional database for the entertainment industry. If you go to www.imdb.com, you can search for any actor, writer, director (or member of any other craft in TV or film) and find their professional credits. This is useful for entertainment industry professionals as they can instantly look up someone's resume (particularly helpful for casting directors). It is also the place where viewers can look up what movies and TV shows their favorite actors have been in.

One of the cool services IMDB.com provides is what is called the STARmeter. (This particular tool received some criticism earlier in 2014, but for the example I am using here, it should be just fine.) The STARmeter aggregates all of the searches on IMDB.com that people are doing on a weekly basis all around the world (this is in the millions), plus a handful of other factors, and ranks every actor that has ever been on television or in the movies on a relative basis, from the most famous (Ranking #1) to those bit players who might have appeared once and are now wholly forgotten (a ranking of #500,000 or below).

If you chart STARmeter's weekly listings over time, you come up with something that looks a lot like a stock chart. And by looking at this "stock chart of the actor," you can very clearly see the ups and downs inherent in every actor's career, as well as their relative popularity to every other actor who is currently listed. The Number One slot is often held by names like Brad Pitt and Leonardo DiCaprio.

My chart vacillates wildly between about 5,000 (when I am on a currently airing TV series) and 50,000 (when I have not worked in a while). You could say I am like a volatile small-cap stock, whereas Brad and Leonardo are blue chips!

If you have done work in the film or television arena, you should look yourself up on IMDB.com and see how you rank. It is an interesting study in how well you are doing professionally (at least based on public popularity).

While an exercise like this doesn't really help predict where your artistic career will go in the future (any more than a stock chart can really predict future profits), it does serve to illustrate the value of artistic work over time, or at least the impact of the artist's efforts upon the culture. The spikes on my STARmeter chart, for instance, represent the culmination of years of investing my creative time to improve myself as an actor so that I was ready for the challenge of a weekly TV series when it came.

It is unfortunate that there is not a reliable empirical instrument in other fields that could help measure the impact of one's artistic efforts in graphic ways. In a certain sense, social media can fill a similar function. But again, a social network that is robust enough to provide useable feedback and connection with an audience broad enough to impact the trajectory of your career is almost always the result of years of investment on the part of the artist.

Here is the definition of Time Value of Money from http://www.investopedia.com/terms/t/timevalueofmoney.asp:

"The idea that money available at the present time is worth more than the same amount in the future due to its potential earning capacity. This core principle of finance holds that, provided money can earn interest, any amount of money is worth more the sooner it is received."

A fundamental principal of sound investing is the time value of money ("TMV"). From the perspective of planning your creative life, it means whatever you do with your time should have the potential to pay some kind of return that is greater than if you had used that time for some other activity in the present.

One of the things that the STARmeter charts I just discussed illustrates in a graphic way is the timeframe involved in a long and committed professional career in the arts. Look at the spikes and valleys of almost any actor's STARmeter chart and you will see volatility (radical movements up and down). So, if you are planning to go into the arts as a profession, or you are thinking about your next career move or rebirth, consider the value of time in your decision-making process. First, how much time are you willing to invest in any particular artistic endeavor? And second, how long are you willing to wait to accomplish your goals? In the end, how you invest your creative time and for how long you invest it will directly affect your return in terms of satisfaction from your artistic life.

Diversifying Your Artistic Portfolio

"Art is the output of thoughtful creative expression through available external mediums." – Kevin Page

I think of art as creative expression. The way that creative expression is communicated to others (its "form" or "medium") is sort of irrelevant. Each medium, of course, has to be mastered, and some mediums are very difficult to work in. Take, for instance, the pointillist painting style or the demands of performing Kabuki Theater. But in the end, art is really just art, and the adjudicating factor in whether it is "good" art or not should be whether it is done with love and passion and skill by the artist. This is why I have always felt equally comfortable acting on the stage or describing a painting I've created.

But I want to go further. In many ways the idea of a medium of expression can be extended to other activities or human endeavors. For instance, business, sales, mathematics, teaching, engineering, even a legal argument can all be viewed as types of creative expression and therefore art; so can customer service, nursing care, and traffic directing (when done with style and aplomb). I believe that writing a screenplay or writing a business plan can both be crowning achievements of the artistic mind (at least when done well), but let me take this even further: Most every pursuit can be artistically driven.

In the universe of creativity, there are fundamental rules of order, just like there are in the physical Universe. One such rule is that all forms of artistic achievement take TIME regardless of their medium of expression. This means that any creative activity you engage in is going to require a direct INVESTMENT of your time. So if we can look at an artistic endeavor as an investment asset (of your time, at a minimum), how can we manage that asset to provide the most satisfactory return profile over its useable lifetime? In other words, if I have only so much time to invest in artistic pursuits, how do I most wisely invest that time as if it were money? You would rather own stocks that go up over time than down, wouldn't you? Well, it's the same way with creativity. You would probably much rather be spending your time on things that pay dividends during your creative (and financial) lifetime than projects that suck up your time and go nowhere in the end.

Creativity As an Investable Asset

I have a very unique background. Off-and-on for more than 30 years I have been a full-time actor, making my living in American movies, TV shows, on the stage, in commercials for both TV and radio, and as a corporate spokesman and educator. During that same period, often for stretches of years at a time, I developed other careers for myself, in part to make a living and in part because, unless I'm actually working on a set as an actor, I tend to get bored with all of the waiting and the down-time.

My extended résumé includes such non-acting professions as television writer, stockbroker, video editor, marketing executive, business consultant, festival promoter, inventor, public speaker, novelist, municipal financial advisor, documentary filmmaker, fine art oil painter, and FINRA-registered investment banker.

You will notice that my list of career pursuits is diverse. I have done a lot of very different things. And not all of these fields made money for me at the time. In some cases, I've established entire careers that ended up being only a way to get to the next opportunity. But, if you take this crazy mix of industry and arts and lay it out on a piece of paper in a kind of flow chart, you can start to see certain patterns emerge.

Five Investment Principals for Your Creative Time

During my time as a financial consultant for the Wall Street powerhouse firm, Smith Barney, I would advise clients on how to build a basic financial portfolio of diversified assets based on their personal life goals and time-horizons. To do this, we would build an investment plan where we would list all of the client's assets (cash, house, retirement accounts, etc.) and all of their goals for a particular timeframe (usually "retirement" at some distant point in the future). For this thought exercise, take a look at all of the creative time and creative engagements in your life and your goals as a serial creative over a period of time you deem reasonable. (Remember you are investing your time, not day-trading it, so make your timeframes reasonably long; think years not weeks.)

Here are 5 very simple ways, drawn from the financial world, to look at your creative time like a stock investment:

1) Analyze. Look at how you spend all the time in your day (don't forget evenings and weekends.) Where do you spend the most creative hours per week? Where should you be spending more?

2) Buy right. In the stock market, the timing of when you invest your money can make all the difference between successes and losses. You want to think about the timing of when-you-do-what with your creative career.

3) <u>Diversify</u>. If you are not already doing so, figure out ways to spend your creative energy on multiple different projects over different timeframes.

4) <u>Know when to sell</u>. Successful portfolio investors often have a disciplined sell strategy guiding when to take profits and move on to some other investment (hopefully avoiding loss.) Do this with your artistic pursuits. If one activity is costing you a lot of time and not moving you forward (or worse yet, making you feel bad about yourself) dump it! Hit the "sell" button. If your time investment is not working, rebalance your portfolio.

5) <u>Leverage</u>. If you are involved in multiple artistic and business pursuits, you may find opportunities for those engagements to cross-fertilize. If you are a published author, this may help you get paid speaking gigs. If you've been an actor, you may be able to get invited to a fan convention (this can be quite lucrative). Maybe your singing career leads to invitations in business. I always look for ways to leverage my contacts from one area to another.

Invest Your Creative Time Wisely

The fundamental point is that your time is an asset (just like investment capital or cash), and it can be consciously managed. How can you diversify your creative activities? Is your current job a creative activity for you? Or are you looking to build a career in the future? If you are thinking of changing careers, I definitely think it is worth going through the process of analyzing your creative time and quantifying just what your time assets are? Then you can make some informed decisions based on allocating that time in a way you think gives you the most upside potential.

Working with Stars

I have worked on-camera with Robert De Niro, Billy Bob Thornton, George Clooney, Pierce Brosnan, Linda Gray, Patrick Duffy, Jeff Daniels (twice), Jason Patric, Jean Claude Van Damme, Chuck Norris, Carol O'Connor, Christopher Reeve, Dolph Lundgren, David Hasselhoff, Susan Lucci, Wishbone (the dog), and others.

As an actor, I am considered a specialist. I am a character actor, which means that in one way or another I have passed beyond being good looking into the realm of "having an interesting face"; and after a 30-year career in front of the cameras, I'm mostly hired to work directly with stars or other celebrities to make them look good. Such a position bears a couple of different responsibilities beyond just knowing your lines when you get to the set:

A. You had better be very, VERY good when you show up to work with a star of high caliber or they will blow you off the screen! If you are not full-out amazing, your character will receive little or no camera coverage in the editing (all of that will go to the star) and the writers will immediately begin looking for ways to write you out of future episodes!

B) It is very difficult to avoid becoming a sycophant around gigantic personalities ... BUT YOU BETTER NOT DO IT! Under no (or at least very few) circumstances should you kiss ass on the star or otherwise behave out of the ordinary. If they want to see fans, they can step outside of their trailer. YOU are there to work with them professionally, and that is a whole different ball of wax from asking for autographs or photos on your iPhone. And your work affects their work. So be professional. Be polite. But do not suck up or ask for autographs (even when others are doing so). You won't stand out as a competent co-worker and someone to be trusted if you make yourself part of the fan-crowd. So, hold your own or get out of the way, but don't be "that guy" on a set.

C) Be funny/clever or serious/smart (although funny/clever usually works best), but don't be boring or overly talkative. Larry Hagman and Billy Bob Thornton are two of the funniest human beings I have ever met in person. Both of them possess a charisma and a wit that simply light up a room. Even if they weren't internationally famous, they would have still had the same effect on a group of people. Their personalities are literally magnetic, and that's one of the reasons they are stars in the first place. So, if you can be funny (in an appropriate way) on the set and get a laugh or two of your own, this will help everyone deal with the tension that's inherent on a film or television set. I grew up as a class clown (as many actors did) and so I try to land the occasional punch line. It doesn't always work (and you can certainly blow yourself up this way); but if you are lucky, people (including the star) will think you are funny and a good actor. On the other hand, a guy like Jason Patric is generally a very serious fellow (at least when he is working, off set he actually has a wicked sense of humor too). With someone like Jason, I am all business. I sit quietly in my chair until it's time to go before the camera, maintaining a certain level of concentration (like meditation) at all times while I'm on the set with him. So you have to know which way to go and when: funny/clever or serious/smart. If you don't know which to choose, stay quiet.

D) Always give it your all on the other guy's coverage (particularly when it is on the star) and be ready to do your own best job *last*. Currently, the expected protocol is to stay present, focused, and give full and committed reactions even when you are not on camera. And I think that goes for stars, too. At least that's what all the stars that I respect do. Patrick Duffy is a master at this.

He very consistently is right there with you, during his co-stars close-ups just as much as his own; a super-generous guy. However, here's a practical reality of Hollywood: Usually, the star's close-ups are first and the guest character actor or co-star goes last. So, no matter how long the day, an actor worth his scale will still have enough energy left at the very end to knock his close-up out of the park—otherwise, that coverage will go to the star as explained above.

The rest of the time, when I'm not on set and directly in a scene with the star, I leave them alone (unless I am invited to engage in conversation or otherwise hang out.) This is a rule you will certainly be taught as an extra and already should know if you are hired professionally in a speaking role for film or TV. But I also respect this rule when I'm credited as a bona fide guest star or above. There are reasons for this:

Try to imagine that your job on any particular day requires you to go through the emotions of losing your family and your marriage, being chased by police, getting into an argument with a criminal then getting into a fight with him, or any other set of circumstances that might make up the character arc of the star of a TV series or movie. This is fairly serious stuff even though it is "just acting." The way this is often accomplished is to simply go through the actual emotions of the circumstances of the scene. Even if you don't really get hurt, the body doesn't necessarily know the difference between "real" and "fake" screaming, crying, shouting, slapping, being slapped, shooting an automatic weapon or being in close proximity to the fireball from a multi-story explosion. It is intense. It can give you real rushes of adrenaline. If done well, the emotions are real. It can be exhausting. And if you are the star of a show, you are most likely going through some version of this every day for weeks on end (or at least being prepared to do so).

In general, this is why you want to leave these people alone unless you are directly engaged in the work being done. They really need to concentrate! Be friendly and smile. Be nice to everyone on the set. But otherwise do your job and mostly be quiet about it. You will know if you ever reach a position to violate any of these rules. Until then, make your momma proud and be politely seen and not heard.

The final note is this: even if you are not on set with a well-known star, take care of your crew. Be polite. Be kind. Listen. They are there to help you look good. They are also the very first audience for your performance (as they are for every scene in the show), so treat them well and do whatever you can to "be liked" by the crew.

13 CODA: A DAY IN THE LIFE (PART TWO)

My book is complete. I have received the copy-corrected draft back from my editor and will send it off to the publishers later this week after one more final read through. However, I always like books (particularly my own) to have some kind of happy ending, even if they are nonfiction like this one. So…

As I write these final words, I am sitting in a hotel room in a city that is not my home. Tomorrow morning, bright and early, a van will pull up to the lobby of my hotel and transport me to a location set where I will perform a couple of scenes with a world famous movie star before catching a plane back home again tomorrow night.

You might have guessed by the tone of the story in Chapter Three (A Day in the Life of an Actor) that I was *not* cast in any of the roles that I auditioned for that day. The competition was high (and I blew my lines in both of the commercial readings!), so it was someone else's turn to win the roles on the TV series that time and I got nothing for my $600 worth of travel expenses. If you are going to be a pro in this business, you simply must be able to deal with disappointment.

To put a positive spin on that whole story, I might point out that at least I gave good solid readings for the TV show and I *could* have been cast based on the auditions I delivered. I also delivered those auditions under extreme pressure (remember I had to re-shoot the one I "nailed" the first time) and the casting director was aware of it. So I might have earned a few brownie points for that (remember my rule about always being nice to everyone, including the casting assistants when they give you bad news!).

Here's what actually happened.

That whole series of events took place on a single day just before Christmas. By the time I took off for the holidays, it was pretty clear that I had not been cast on any of those projects and I put all of that behind me and celebrated an otherwise excellent year with my family (I had, after all, completed four books for publication in a single year!).

On January 4th of the brand new year, as my editor was reviewing the text you have just read, I got an email from my agent. The producers of the television show that I had auditioned for, while they had not cast me in the episode I read for, liked my work and had decided to hire me (without another audition) for a recurring guest star role on their series. This was actually a better deal than either of the other two roles I had been up for.

The moral of this story, if there is one, is that the actor's life is always (and always will be) hectic, unpredictable, and fraught with stressors beyond your control. That is just how show business is. But how you deal with that reality is basically your choice. If you learn to meditate and use the other confidence-building practices I have shared with you in this book, you will undoubtedly learn to deal with that stress and uncertainty in a different, more balanced, more healthy way. It just takes a little practice.

Practice mindfulness, be a diamond, and hopefully we

will meet while working together on a set or stage someday!

OTHER BOOKS BY KEVIN PAGE

Advanced Consciousness Training for Actors (Routledge Press, Fall, 2018) explores theories and techniques for deepening the individual actor's capacity to concentrate and focus attention. Going well beyond the common exercises found in actor training programs, these practices utilize consciousness expanding "technologies" derived from both Eastern and Western traditions of meditation and mindfulness training as well as more recent discoveries from the fields of psychology and neuroscience. This book reviews the scientific literature on consciousness studies and mindfulness research to discover techniques for focusing attention, expanding self-awareness, and increasing levels of mental concentration—all foundational skills of the performing artist in any medium.

Psychology for Actors (Routledge Press, Fall, 2018) is the first book-length study of modern psychology, specifically designed for the working actor and actor-in-training, that covers discrete areas of psychological theory from a perspective that actors can understand and use in their creative process.

"What is my character's motivation?" While this question is perhaps a caricature of the earnest actor's quest for realistic performance, it is also a serious psychological investigation. ALL contemporary actors, whether on stage, film, or television, go to at least some lengths in exploring or making psychological choices about the characters they play. But what psychology do they use in making their judgments? Is it the behaviorism or Freudian psychoanalysis of the 1940s and 1950s? The "pop" psychology of the 1960s humanistic movement? Cognitive neuroscience? The personality theories of Adler, Erikson, or Jung? What about psychological types such as introverted and extroverted? Abnormal or positive psychology? Put another way, how much actual psychology does the average actor really know and use?

Psychology for Actors is an essential addition to every actor's and director's personal library and an indispensable reference tool for creative work in any medium: stage, screen, and beyond.

ABOUT THE AUTHOR

Kevin Page is an author, actor, and holds a Master's degree in psychology. He writes about mindfulness meditation and other healthful mind/body training techniques. He was blown away by a robot (ED-209) in the classic movie *RoboCop* (1987), offered Jerry his "show about nothing" on *Seinfeld*, and played the character who ultimately shot and killed J. R. Ewing on the 2012 re-boot of the TV series *Dallas*. Throughout his 35-year acting career, Page has appeared in over 200 commercials, voice overs, stage plays, and industrial films. Plus, he has two books coming out in 2018: *Advanced Consciousness Training (A.C.T.) for Actors* (Routledge, 2018), which teaches both stage and screen actors how to use various meditative arts to improve their abilities as performers; and *Psychology for Actors* (Routledge, 2018), which applies 20th century post-Stanislavski psychological theories and techniques to the actor's craft. In addition to writing and acting, Page has been a documentary filmmaker, stockbroker, investment banker, entrepreneur, gallery owner, and artist. He holds four U. S. patents on a technology that uses robotics and software to create large-format pointillist-style oil paintings.

Kevin Page is active on social media and can be followed on various platforms, including:

www.KevinPage.com

www.ACTforActors.blog

Twitter: @KevinWPage

IMDB Profile: www.imdb.com/name/nm0656241/

YouTube Channel:
https://www.youtube.com/user/kpbarnum

Made in the USA
Columbia, SC
09 February 2022

55775999R00091